Theodore Roosevelt

UP*close:*

Theodore Roosevelt

a twentieth-century life by
MICHAEL L. COOPER

VIKING

VIKING
Published by Penguin Group
Penguin Young Readers Group, 345 Hudson Street, New York, New York 10014, U.S.A.
Penguin Group (Canada), 90 Eglinton Avenue East, Suite 700, Toronto, Ontario,
Canada M4P 2Y3 (a division of Pearson Penguin Canada Inc.)
Penguin Books Ltd, 80 Strand, London WC2R 0RL, England
Penguin Ireland, 25 St Stephen's Green, Dublin 2, Ireland (a division of Penguin Books Ltd)
Penguin Group (Australia), 250 Camberwell Road, Camberwell, Victoria 3124, Australia
(a division of Pearson Australia Group Pty Ltd)
Penguin Books India Pvt Ltd, 11 Community Centre, Panchsheel Park, New Delhi – 110 017, India
Penguin Group (NZ), 67 Apollo Drive, Rosedale, North Shore 0632, New Zealand
(a division of Pearson New Zealand Ltd)
Penguin Books (South Africa) (Pty) Ltd, 24 Sturdee Avenue, Rosebank, Johannesburg 2196,
South Africa

Penguin Books Ltd, Registered Offices: 80 Strand, London WC2R 0RL, England

First published in 2009 by Viking, a division of Penguin Young Readers Group

10 9 8 7 6 5 4 3 2 1

Text copyright © Michael L. Cooper, 2009
Photo credits:
Pages 14, 25, 50, 63, 70, 102–103, 112, 121, 141, 154, 162: Theodore Roosevelt Collection,
Harvard College Library
Page 129: Courtesy U.S. Department of the Interior
Page 185: Library of Congress

LIBRARY OF CONGRESS CATALOGING-IN-PUBLICATION DATA IS AVAILABLE
ISBN: 978-0-670-01134-6

Printed in the U.S.A.   Set in Goudy   Book design by Jim Hoover

To three professors who nurtured
my love of history: John Duncan,
Dan Carter, and Alan Brinkley

✳ CONTENTS ✳

FOREWORD

FOR TWENTY YEARS I've been wanting to write about Theodore Roosevelt. This author, big-game hunter, conservationist, explorer, historian, naturalist, rancher, reformer, soldier, and twenty-sixth president of the United States appeals to me on many levels.

As someone who grew up camping and hunting, I understand the pleasure that Roosevelt, a New Yorker, found sleeping under the stars on the Dakota prairie or tramping through the Maine woods. And going out west to become a rancher as Roosevelt did was one of my childhood fantasies.

He and I both fell in love with books at a young age. As an adult he read nearly a book a day, while also writing thirty-eight of his own. And what book lover wouldn't admire a man who as president plucked the great poet Edwin Arlington Robinson out of poverty and gave him a government job with instructions to write lots of poems?

I also identify with the illness that robbed Roosevelt of so much of a regular childhood. My own health problems kept me out of school and in a hospital or convalescing for a year, reshaping my adolescence. I envy Roosevelt his loving family, whose support gave him the determination to overcome his illness.

Even though people seemed to forget it at times, Roosevelt was human and had his faults. He was self-centered and self-righteous. With his children he could be overbearing. And he could be unbearably preachy about morals and personal behavior. People of color, Roosevelt believed, weren't as "advanced" as Anglo-Saxons. While he was a man of great courage, it was at times a foolhardy courage that made him flirt needlessly with danger, as though challenging death. And as a government official Roosevelt could bend the truth or the law when it suited his purposes. He did this in the months before the Spanish-American War, which made him a national hero, and when he secured the Panama Canal, which he considered one of his greatest achievements.

Of course, few of us would know anything about

Roosevelt if he had not been president. Throughout most of his life, America was undergoing a dizzying transformation from a nation of farms and small towns to a nation of fast-growing cities like Chicago, Pittsburgh, and Detroit and huge corporations such as Standard Oil and U.S. Steel, which possessed more wealth and power than many countries. There was a succession of lackluster presidents after the Civil War who were unable or unwilling to face the new challenges of governing. At the beginning of the twentieth century along came Roosevelt. With enormous energy, magnetic personality, and extraordinary intelligence, he was the hero America needed.

INTRODUCTION

JOHN SHRANK HAD been stalking Theodore Roosevelt for three weeks. Roosevelt was running for an unprecedented third term as president of the United States. On October 14, 1912, standing less than ten yards from the candidate outside the Hotel Gilpatrick in Milwaukee, Wisconsin, Shrank shot Roosevelt with a .38 pistol. The bullet pierced his overcoat, steel spectacles case, and a thick copy of a speech folded in his breast pocket before lodging between his ribs. The impact knocked Roosevelt back, but he didn't fall. "As I did not cough up blood I was pretty sure the wound was not a fatal one," he later explained.

"Stand back," Roosevelt yelled as the crowd seized his assailant. "Don't hurt that man." He wanted to see who had tried to kill him. Roosevelt stared into

Shrank's eyes for several seconds before turning aside.

The gunman later said President William McKinley's ghost had told him to kill Roosevelt. McKinley had been assassinated eleven years earlier and Vice President Roosevelt had become president. McKinley's ghost said the vice president had been the assassin. Shrank spent the rest of his life in a mental institution.

Instead of rushing to the hospital, the wounded candidate insisted on going to the Milwaukee Auditorium, where he was scheduled to speak. He was greeted there, as he was everywhere, by a large, cheering crowd. "Friends," he said from the podium, "I shall ask you to be as quiet as possible. I don't know whether you fully understand that I have just been shot; but it takes more than that to kill a Bull Moose." The crowd gasped and then fell silent.

Roosevelt unbuttoned his vest to reveal his bloody shirt. Taking his fifty-page speech out of his coat pocket, he held it up, explaining, "There is a bullet—there is where the bullet went through—and it probably saved me from it going into my heart. The bullet is in me now, so that I cannot make a long speech, but I will try my best. . . . I have altogether too important things to think of to feel any concern over my own death; and now I cannot speak to you insincerely within five minutes of being shot . . . my concern is for many other things. It is not in the least for my own life. . . . No man has had a happier life than I have led."

$\star$ $\star$ **1** $\star$ $\star$

THE STORY OF one of America's greatest presidents, Theodore Roosevelt, begins with his father.

"I owe everything," he once said, "I have or am to Father." His father was Theodore Roosevelt Sr., but the family called him Thee. He was a handsome man with broad shoulders, blue eyes, a square jaw, and chestnut brown hair and beard. Thee was the youngest of five children, all sons, born to Cornelius Van Schaack Roosevelt.

According to an 1858 magazine article, Cornelius was one of New York City's ten bona fide millionaires. He was both rich and old New York. His Dutch ancestors settled on Manhattan Island in 1649 when it was

Theodore, age eight, 1866.

the Dutch colony of New Amsterdam. Cornelius made the family's fortune in the 1830s by investing in real estate, which afforded his sons comfortable livings.

At age nineteen, while visiting Georgia, Thee fell in love with a southern belle four years younger than he was named Martha "Mittie" Bulloch. The Bullochs, an old and prominent family, lived north of Atlanta in a white-columned mansion on a plantation worked by slaves. Three years after they met, in 1853, Thee and Mittie married and settled into a town house, a wedding present from his father, on East 20th Street in Manhattan.

Thee and his brother James managed the family's extensive real estate holdings and plate-glass importing company, but the family business wasn't his main focus. "He was interested in every social reform movement," young Theodore recalled, "and he did an immense amount of practical charitable work himself." Thee devoted much of his time to helping poor kids in the Children's Aid Society and similar organizations. He also helped found two major New York institutions, the American Museum of Natural History and the Metropolitan Museum of Art.

In their first eight years of marriage Thee and Mittie had two girls and two boys. They named the first child Anna, but called her "Bamie," short for bambina. No one in the family was called by his or her given name. When the future president was born four years later, October 27, 1858, his parents called him Teedie, which was pronounced *T.D.* The third child, Elliott, was born sixteen months afterward and called Ellie. And Corinne, nineteen months younger than Elliott, was called Conie. All of them except Bamie eventually outgrew their nicknames.

The Roosevelt children were privileged in all ways except good health. Bamie, Thee's favorite, had a spinal defect. As a child she wore an iron brace and as an adult had a slight hunch in her shoulders. Elliott had convulsions, perhaps epilepsy, that caused him to black out, and he was an alcoholic before he was an adult. The youngest, Corinne, had mild asthma.

As for Teedie, "nobody seemed to think I would live." He was a frail, undersized child with large blue eyes that never seemed focused on anything. He suffered almost daily from headaches and diarrhea, which the family delicately referred to with a made-up

Latin-sounding term, *cholera morbus*. But Teedie's most serious problem was asthma.

No one at the time knew what caused asthma or how to stop the frequent attacks that often came at night and lasted hours or days. They made Teedie feel as though he was drowning, and he constantly gasped for breath. Afterward he would be drenched in sweat and exhausted.

It was Teedie's father who often comforted him during these attacks. "I could breathe, I could sleep, when he had me in his arms."

Doctors weren't much help, but one recommended plenty of fresh air and exercise. You "have the mind, but you have not the body," Thee told his son, "and without the help of the body the mind cannot go as far as it should. You must make your body. It is hard drudgery to make one's body, but I know you will do it." Teedie, always eager for his father's approval, vowed he would. This was the beginning of his lifelong devotion to vigorous exercise, which included hiking, boxing, and, in the early 1870s when the family built a new mansion uptown on 57th Street, lifting weights in his own gym. Exercise and being outdoors did appear to improve Teedie's health. As he got older, he became more robust and his asthma bothered him much less.

At about the same time he began exercising, Teedie was cured of another affliction, nearsightedness. One day he realized he was the only one who couldn't read large letters on a billboard. Soon afterward, Teedie happily wrote in the journal he kept, I "got my first pair of spectacles, which literally opened a new world to me. I had no idea how beautiful the world was until I got those spectacles."

Teedie's earliest memories were of the worst crisis the United States had faced in its eighty-five-year existence—the Civil War. Mittie's brothers fought for the Confederacy, so she persuaded Thee not to join the Union Army. Like many affluent Northerners, he hired a substitute to fight. But for the remainder of his life, according to Bamie, her father felt "he had done a very wrong thing" by not putting "every other feeling aside" and fighting for the Union.

The Roosevelt children's friends were either cousins or the children of other wealthy New Yorkers. As a child, Teedie was too frail to hold his own when roughhousing, even with his younger brother. But as an adolescent strengthened by daily exercise, he was fiercely competitive. One year, Teedie noted in his journal, several of the boys held jumping, running, vaulting, wrestling, and boxing contests. There were fifteen events and Teedie won fourteen of them. Although he wasn't a particularly good boxer, he relished the fighting. "If you offered rewards for bloody noses," Teedie told his father, "you would spend a fortune on me alone."

Thee and Mittie educated their children mostly at home. Their first lessons in reading and writing came from Mittie's sister, Aunt Anna, and her mother, Grandmother Bulloch, who both came to live with them in 1856. Later the children had a French governess.

Even before he could read, Teedie discovered books. He was four when he found in his family's library an oversized copy of David Livingstone's *Missionary Travels and Researches in Southern Africa*. For days he dragged it around asking adults to tell him about the colorful illustrations of hippos, zebra, and other exotic animals.

Once he learned to read, Teedie devoured books. He "worshipped *Little Men* and *Little Women*," he recalled, even if they were "girls' stories." He liked boys' books such as Daniel Defoe's *Robinson Crusoe* and Mayne Reid's *The Boy Hunters*, which gave him a "great admiration for men who were fearless and who could hold their own in the world and I had a great desire to be like them."

Teedie also enjoyed *Our Young Folks*, which he pronounced "the very best magazine in the world." He kept copies and reread them even as an adult. The magazine's stories reinforced what Thee and Mittie taught their children about "manliness, decency, and good conduct," and helped Teedie develop strong convictions of right and wrong. The boy didn't like dirty jokes and rarely cursed. Teedie once dropped a friend, he told his father, because "he swore like a trooper." When he was grown, he drank moderately and believed sex was only for married people. A political colleague once said Theodore often acted like he had discovered the Ten Commandments.

While sheltered in many ways, the Roosevelt children saw more of the world than most American children or, for that matter, most adults. Twice Thee took the family on yearlong trips abroad. In 1869, they went on a grand tour of nine European countries.

They first visited Liverpool, England, where Mittie's two unreconstructed brothers lived in exile. Teedie was fascinated by his uncles' exploits during the Civil War. James Dunwoodie Bulloch, a former Confederate admiral, had helped launch the famous Confederate raider, *Alabama*, and his younger brother, Irvine, had been a crew member. Both uncles told Teedie stories about the *Alabama*'s battles, and he would retell them in graphic detail for years afterward. This was probably the best part of the trip for ten-year-old Teedie. He wrote that he "cordially hated" the rest of it.

Teedie had a much better time four years later when the family visited Egypt, Palestine, Syria, Turkey, and Greece. In Egypt the family lived and traveled for three months on a houseboat on the Nile River as they visited such famous sites as the Great Sphinx and the Great Pyramid in Giza. At the end of the tour, the three youngest Roosevelts spent five months with a family in Dresden, Germany, so they could study German and French.

The lack of formal schooling was a problem when

Thee decided he wanted Teedie and Elliott to attend Harvard University. He hired a recent Harvard graduate, Arthur Cutler, to tutor the boys for two years in Greek, Latin, math, and other subjects needed to pass the admission exams. Teedie applied himself to his studies with characteristic zeal, working eight or more hours a day. "The young man never seemed to know what idleness was," his tutored observed, "and every leisure moment would find the last novel, some English classic or some abstruse book on natural history in his hands." Elliott lost interest in his studies and dropped out, but Teedie finished ahead of schedule and easily passed his admission exams. In 1876 he enrolled in Harvard where he was no longer Teedie, but "Roosevelt of New York," or Theodore or Teddy, his least favorite name because it was too informal.

Theodore planned to study "out-of-doors natural history." He had been fascinated by insects, birds, and other animals since age seven when he saw a dead seal on the sidewalk outside a fish market. "That seal filled me with every possible feeling of romance and adventure," he recalled. The boy kept notebooks with sketches and observations of ants, spiders, and beetles.

After receiving his first shotgun as a Christmas present at age fourteen, in the name of science Teedie had killed thousands of birds and small animals. He learned taxidermy—the practice of preparing, stuffing, and mounting the skins of animals to look lifelike—and he usually did the work in his room.

But by his sophomore year, Theodore had lost interest in the natural sciences as a career because Harvard "utterly ignored the possibilities of the faunal naturalist, the outdoor naturalist and observer of nature." He wanted to be in the forest or in the jungle rather than in a laboratory.

When Theodore went home for Christmas he found that his father, who was only forty-six, looked notably older. And he was suffering from severe stomach pain. It turned out to be stomach cancer. On February 9, 1878, Thee died. "I felt as if I had been stunned, or as if part of my life had been taken away," Theodore wrote. He was "the one I loved dearest on earth." For months afterward, Theodore imagined his father was nearby. "I almost feel as if he were present with me," he told his mother. That June in the

Theodore as a student at Harvard.

Presbyterian church near the family's rented summer home at Oyster Bay, New York, Theodore said he saw Thee in a pew "as distinctly as if he were alive."

As his grief subsided, Theodore seemed more determined than ever to please his father. "With the help of my God," he vowed, "I will try to lead such a life as he would have wished." He began thinking seriously about adult responsibilities. "I wonder who my wife will be! 'A rare and radiant maiden,' I hope; one who will be as sweet, pure, and innocent as she is wise," he confided to his diary. "Thank heaven I am at least perfectly pure."

In the autumn of his junior year at Harvard, Theodore fell in love with a lively seventeen-year-old named Alice Lee. She was blond, blue-eyed, and, at five feet six inches, just a little shorter than he was. Her family was rich and old Boston. Immediately smitten, Theodore told Alice, "I care for nothing whatever else but for you." On Valentine's Day of 1880, four months before graduation, the couple announced their engagement. They were married October 27, which was Theodore's twenty-second birthday. The night before the wedding the groom wrote, "My happiness is so great it makes me almost afraid."

The newlyweds moved into Mittie's Manhattan mansion. When they returned to New York in the autumn of 1881 from a five-month honeymoon in Europe, Theodore had to face a problem familiar to many young adults: what to do with his life.

It was curiosity, Theodore later explained, that led him to a saloon on 59th Street and up the stairs to a barnlike room furnished with benches and spittoons. It was the headquarters, "a kind of club-room" Theodore recalled, for the 21st District Republican Association, where lawyers, saloon keepers, horsecar conductors, and tough guys from the tenements spent many of their evenings.

At that time, the Republican and Democratic political parties were a bigger part of men's lives than today. More than three-quarters of all voters belonged to one party or the other. (Today about two-thirds of all voters are affiliated with the two major parties.) In the days before radio, television, movies, and big-league sports, politics, with its passionate speakers and torch light parades at election time, was entertainment. But it was serious as well.

The United States was changing rapidly in the

second half of the nineteenth century. After the Civil War, European immigrants poured into New York, Chicago, Baltimore, and other already large cities, tripling the nation's population. Instead of working on farms or in trades such as blacksmithing or barrel making, more people were working in corporations and factories. Government then didn't regulate businesses or factories to make sure they were safe places to work or inspect food to make sure it was safe to eat. Previous generations of Americans hadn't wanted government services or regulations. But as the United States grew larger and more complex, Americans believed government should try to make day-to-day life safe and orderly. Many political battles were over the role of government.

Theodore complained that too many young people in his crowd in Manhattan and at Harvard felt that public life was beneath them. There was a "deplorable lack of interest in the political questions of the day among respectable, well-educated men." He knew that politics was "rough and brutal and unpleasant to deal with." But, as Theodore wrote in one of his many letters to friends and family, which he often signed TR, he wanted to "be of the governing class."

Theodore hadn't planned on being a candidate for political office when Joe Murray, one of the 21st District Republican Association's leaders, asked him to run for state assembly. Murray thought Theodore's fresh face and prominent name would win votes. Murray was right. The candidate did little campaigning, and he won easily with 3,490 votes to the other guy's 1,989. Although Theodore wouldn't realize it until years later, he had embarked on his life's work.

$\star$ $\star$ 2 $\star$ $\star$

THE IMPRESSION THAT Theodore Roosevelt made when he first appeared as an assemblyman in Albany, New York, was not exactly the kind politicians dream of making.

"Suddenly our eyes . . . became glued on a young man who was coming in through the door," a fellow assemblyman described the first time he saw Theodore. "His hair was parted in the center, and he had sideburns. He wore a single eyeglass, with a gold chain over his ear. He had on a cutaway coat with one button at the top, and the ends of its tails almost reached the tops of his shoes. He carried a gold-headed cane in one hand, a silk hat in the other, and he walked in the bent over fashion that was the style with the young men of the day. His trousers were as tight as a tailor could make them, and had a bell shaped bottom to cover his shoes."

Republicans and Democrats alike in the state capitol immediately dismissed the new guy, who was the assembly's youngest member, as a "society man and a dude" and a "kid glove, scented, silk stocking, poodle-headed, degenerate" aristocrat. The insults and bullying that first term, Theodore recalled, reminded him of being a new boy at school. And he was one new boy who didn't back down from any kind of confrontation.

Theodore, who was five feet eight inches and weighed 140 pounds, stood up to "Big John" McManus, a "huge, fleshy, unutterably coarse and low brute" when he heard the Democratic assemblyman wanted to toss him in a blanket. Blanket tossing is a form of mild hazing in which a group of people hold the edges of a blanket and repeatedly toss their victim high into the air. "By God if you try anything like that," he warned McManus, a former prize fighter, "I'll bite you, I'll kick you in the balls, I'll do anything to you—you'd better leave me alone."

In another incident, on a cold winter evening

Theodore and two colleagues stopped by a popular Albany saloon. A Democratic assemblyman made a wisecrack about the short jacket Theodore was wearing. "Won't Mama's boy catch cold?" Theodore, one of his companions said, flared up and "knocked him down and he got up and he hit him again, and when he got up he hit him again." Maybe it was his thick glasses and slight build, but few people would have guessed the "dude" had begun boxing at age twelve and in his junior year at Harvard had finished second in a boxing championship.

Verbal confrontations were more common for him, though, and Theodore was better with words than fists. He described one Democrat as "either dumb or an idiot; probably both." Democrats of Irish heritage such as John McManus were "a stupid, sodden, vicious lot, most of them being equally deficient in brains and virtue." Theodore used his harshest language on Democrats, but he didn't spare fellow Republicans. About as smart as "an average balloon" is how he described one man. And another was "entirely unprincipled, with the same idea of Public Life and Civil Service that a vulture had of a dead sheep."

Theodore stood out in many ways. He had a laugh that his own mother described as an "ungreased squeak," and when he wanted to speak in the assembly, which was often, his high-pitched, upper-class voice pierced the capitol's cathedral-like chamber, "mister spee-kar, mister spee-kar." In political debates, a colleague explained there "wasn't anything cool about him. He yelled and pounded his desk and when they attacked him, he would fire back with all the venom imaginable. He was the most indiscreet guy I ever met." One journalist noted that Theodore fought tooth and nail with "a trait of ruthless righteousness."

Theodore's energy impressed everyone who knew him. In the Albany boardinghouse where he lived during the week, Assemblyman Billy Hunt recalled, he "would come into the house like a thunder bolt. . . . Such a super-abundance of animal life was hardly ever condensed in a human life."

Because of his energy and combative personality one newspaper called him "the Cyclone Assemblyman." The Cyclone ended his first legislative session by ripping into Judge T. R. Westbrook, a powerful state supreme court justice whose judicial opinions had made wealthy Wall Street businessman Jay Gould even wealthier. In his first major political speech in the assembly, Theodore introduced a resolution to impeach Westbrook.

He had done his homework by pouring over back issues of *The New York Times* and talking for hours with newspaper editors about the judge's career. Theodore saw a letter Westbrook had written to Gould saying he was "willing to go to the very verge of judicial discretion" to protect the businessman's interests. There had been rumors about Judge Westbrook, but corruption was so common in local, state, and national government no one had bothered to investigate until now.

In his speech, Theodore called Gould and his Wall Street cronies "sharks" and "swindlers." They were "men whose financial dishonesty is a matter of common notoriety." It was "of vital importance," he stressed, "that the judiciary of this State shall be beyond reproach."

The speech was "like the bursting of a bombshell," wrote a fellow legislator; "a dead silence fell on the whole assembly." The only sound was Theodore's high-pitched, somewhat stuttering voice and his right fist smacking his left palm as though punctuating his words.

"I have drawn blood," he bragged in a letter to Alice. "It is rather the hit of the season so far, and I think I have made a success of it. Letters and telegrams of congratulations come pouring in from all quarters."

The state's newspapers agreed. The speech had "a boldness that was almost scathing," stated *The New York Sun*. "Mr. Roosevelt accomplished more good than a man of his age and experience has accomplished in years," the *New York Evening Post* declared. He "has a most refreshing habit of calling men and things by their right names, and in these days of judicial, ecclesiastical, and journalistic subserviency to the robber-barons of the [Wall] Street, it needs some little courage in any public man to characterize them and their acts in fitting terms," stated a *New York Times* editorial. The paper's editors predicted "a splendid career" for the assemblyman.

Despite his memorable speech and the editorial praise, Theodore's resolution failed. It was up to a handful of assemblymen on the judiciary committee to determine if there was enough evidence for impeachment. A bare majority of the committee voted no. It was later rumored that someone, probably connected to Gould, had paid several members $2,500 each to vote against impeachment.

It was the robber-baron era when rich businessmen like Gould, J. P. Morgan, and John D. Rockefeller had a public-be-damned attitude as they wheeled and dealed to make as much money as possible. Many of these men lived in New York City, America's largest and wealthiest city. They bribed judges, lawmakers, and government officials to get their way. New York State's capital, wrote one journalist, was "evil and heart sickening . . . a cesspool." Theodore estimated that at least a third of the 128 assembly members sold their votes to the highest bidder.

During the Westbrook hearings, over lunch an old family friend advised Theodore to "leave politics" and take his place "with the right kind of people." Always, the friend explained, there would be an inner circle of businessmen, lawyers, and judges to "control others and obtain the real rewards." This was "the first glimpse I had of that combination between business and politics," Theodore later wrote, "which I was in after years so often to oppose."

Even if the family friend didn't approve of Theodore's work, many people did. Americans, weary of dishonest politicians and arrogant businessmen, applauded his attacks on corruption. He was our "ideal," said a Harvard classmate. "We hailed him as the dawn of a new era."

DESPITE THE PRAISE he had received that first year in the assembly, Theodore felt ambivalent about his work. "I have become a political hack," he informed a friend. "But don't think I am going into politics after this year, for I am not."

Money might have been a concern, because as an assemblyman he earned just $1,500 a year. Thee had left each of his children $125,000, which was a substantial sum at a time when many people earned less than $1,000 a year. But Theodore was spending his inheritance quickly. There was $2,500 for Alice's wedding presents; five expensive months in Europe; a town house on Manhattan's West 45th Street; the cost of going out nearly every night to the opera, the theater, or dinner; and the $20,000 he had paid for ninety-six acres of land on Long Island's North Shore, near Oyster Bay, where he planned to spend nearly as much building a huge home.

Theodore had taken a few law courses over the past two years at Columbia University. He enjoyed the classroom arguments, but he was disappointed because "the teachings of the law-books and of the classroom seemed to me to be against justice." Theodore's first book, *The Naval War of 1812*, which he began writing at Harvard, was published in the spring of 1882 to acclaim in both Great Britain and the United States. He liked writing, but not enough to do it full time.

In the fall of 1882, Theodore changed his mind and decided to run for another term in the assembly. It's not clear what made him change his mind, but he enjoyed the rough and tumble of politics as well as the attention and praise. In the November election he won by a bigger margin, 2,200 votes, than in his first election. Unlike the previous year, his Republican colleagues didn't laugh at him when they convened in January. Instead, they nominated Theodore to be speaker of the assembly, one of the most powerful political positions in the state. But the Democrats held the majority, so naturally they elected one of their own members to be speaker. For a twenty-four-year-old, second-term assemblyman, just receiving the nomination was quite an honor.

Each Monday morning that winter Theodore reluctantly left Alice in Manhattan for the 145-mile train trip upstate to Albany. "I felt as if my heart would break when I left my own little pink darling," he wrote on one lonely Monday evening in the capital. After a long day of work, even when the temperature was well below freezing, he unwound by taking brisk ten- to fifteen-mile walks around the old Dutch city, or by hiring a boxer to come to his room to spar.

During the 1883 session, one of Theodore's favorite targets was the "wealthy criminal class," a term he used in a speech in 1883 and one of the many memorable phrases he coined. He was speaking of people such as Jay Gould, whom he called "the arch thief of Wall Street," and other rich businessmen who pursued profit with little regard for the law or public welfare. And he led a group of assemblymen, who were dubbed Roosevelt Republicans, to defeat several bills giving special favors to corporations. Theodore battled both

Democrats and Republicans, whose comfortable careers depended on pleasing businessmen.

Theodore's dislike for rich businessmen didn't mean he felt sympathy for ordinary working people. He voted against bills to reduce the workday for New York City streetcar conductors to twelve hours, against giving pensions to teachers, and against increasing firemen's salaries to $100 a month. The assemblyman felt the city couldn't afford such benefits.

One of Theodore's biggest legislative accomplishments that second session was to team up with New York Democratic governor Grover Cleveland to establish a civil service commission to protect state government jobs from political interference. It was common for politicians to award government jobs to people who supported them rather than to people who had the necessary skills to do the jobs. New York State's civil service commission, which was similar to one that Congress had created that year for the federal government, was a major first step in making government more stable and more efficient.

At the end of the legislative session, newspapers

again praised his fearlessness, honesty, and independence. Theodore himself said he "rose like a rocket." It was the beginning, wrote one of his biographers, of "a political ascent without parallel in American history." Life was good, and it was getting better.

In the summer of 1883, Theodore and Alice heard the best news a young couple could hope for: they were going to have a baby. The first, they hoped, of many children. But being an expectant father wasn't enough to keep him at home.

Theodore's asthma had been particularly bad that summer, and he used it as an excuse to go west to hunt buffalo. After a seventeen-hundred-mile trip to the Dakota Territory, he got off the train in a frontier town called Little Missouri, where he hired a hunting guide and horses to take him into the region that Indians and early explorers called the badlands. In one of his letters home, TR described the land as "a very desolate place . . . high, barren hills, scantily clad with coarse grass, and here and there in sheltered places a few stunted cotton wood trees; 'wash-outs,' deepening at times into great canyons, and steep cliffs of the most curious formation."

Just a few years earlier, tens of thousands of buffalo had roamed the grassy prairie in the Dakota and nearby Montana territories. But white people pushing their way west had slaughtered nearly all of them. Theodore hunted for over a week with little other than bad luck. Nearly every day they were soaked by a cold rain. His horse threw him. While crawling through brush to get a good shot at a deer, he nearly crawled over a rattlesnake. Twice he shot at buffalo, but he missed and they galloped away. Yet he thought it was all fun.

"I am now feeling very well and am enjoying the life very much," one of TR's letters to Alice reported. "Of course I am dirty," a later letter added, "in fact I have not taken off my clothes for two weeks, not even at night, except for one bath in the river, but I sleep, eat and work as I never could do in ten years time in the city."

After a week and a half Theodore finally shot a buffalo. It weighed nearly two thousand pounds, by far the largest creature he had ever killed. The happy hunter danced around the dead animal and then rewarded his amused guide with a $100 tip. "Hurrah! The luck has turned at last," he informed Alice. "I will bring you home the head of a great buffalo bull."

Another letter had more news. Theodore had given two men whom he had just met a check for $14,000 to buy a small ranch and four hundred head of cattle, which they would graze for him on government-owned grasslands. Now that the buffalo were nearly gone and the Indians were confined to reservations, raising cattle was becoming big business on the Great Plains. And it was fashionable for wealthy men from the East and from Europe to own cattle ranches. One local rancher was a young French nobleman. Theodore justified his hasty investment by saying it would provide a good income while leaving him time for public service.

The last of the letters from this trip concluded, "This has been by all odds the pleasantest and most successful trip I have ever made." Years later he would say that it was in the Dakota Badlands where "the romance of my life began."

That November voters in the 21st District reelected Theodore to a third term, and Republicans statewide won a majority of seats in the assembly. Eager to be speaker, Theodore tirelessly crisscrossed the state asking his fellow assemblymen for their votes. But when the assembly convened in Albany at the beginning of 1884, the Republican Old Guard showed it didn't trust the independent young politician and elected another speaker.

A few weeks later, on a Wednesday in mid-February, Theodore received a telegram that Alice had given birth the night before to a daughter. They had already agreed if the baby was a girl to name her Alice Lee. The new father, no doubt enjoying the hearty back-slapping and handshakes from the other assemblymen, planned to catch a late train into the city. But then a second telegram arrived. Alice, who was staying at his mother's home, was seriously ill. Theodore took the next train south to Manhattan and, after what must have been a painfully long trip, arrived at his mother's house on 57th Street near midnight. "There is a curse on this house," Elliott told him. "Mother is dying, and Alice is dying too."

Everyone thought Mittie had been sick with a bad cold, but it turned out to be typhoid fever. At three

A.M. Thursday she died. Eleven hours later, just as a thick fog over the city began to lift, Alice died. The cause was a kidney ailment called Bright's disease. It was Valentine's Day, exactly four years after they had announced their engagement. His journal entry for February 14, 1884, was a large cross.

The family held a double funeral at the Fifth Avenue Presbyterian Church. Just like Thee's funeral six years earlier, more than two thousand of the city's most prominent people filled the church. But this time there were two rosewood coffins side by side surrounded by roses and lilies of the field. "Theodore is in a dazed, stunned state," observed his old tutor Arthur Cutler. "He does not know what he does or says." Afterward, before putting his journal aside for several months, Theodore wrote, "For joy or for sorrow my life has now been lived out."

The following week, after entrusting his newborn daughter to Bamie, who lived in a town house on Madison Avenue, Theodore returned to Albany to fill his days, his thoughts, with work. To one friend he explained, "I shall go mad if I were not employed."

The assemblyman had promised his constituents

that he would attack political corruption such as New York City's Tammany Hall, the nation's largest and most notorious political machine. Political machines were unofficial organizations that controlled political life in cities and states. Tammany was a force in New York City politics for about a century. Its most notorious leader was William M. Tweed, who was popularly known as Boss Tweed. He ran Tammany Hall when Theodore was a child. Boss Tweed was convicted in the early 1870s of stealing $100 million of taxpayer money, and he died in prison. But Tammany Hall lived on under new leadership.

Many of the city's twenty-four aldermen and the officials they appointed were puppets for Tammany Hall. Theodore's biggest accomplishment in the assembly was passing the Reform Charter Bill, dubbed the "Roosevelt bill," which gave the city's mayor more power over political appointments. "Tammany Defeated: Mr. Roosevelt's Brilliant Assault on Corruption," lauded a headline in the *New York Herald*.

After the assembly's session ended, Theodore stepped briefly into the spotlight of national politics. He was one of New York State's seventy-four delegates who attended the Republican National Convention in Chicago that June to nominate a candidate for president. Most of the convention's delegates supported former secretary of state James G. Blaine, who was challenging the Republican incumbent Chester A. Arthur.

Both Blaine and Arthur, Theodore believed, represented business as usual, political machines, patronage, and corruption. With his new friend Massachusetts politician Henry Cabot Lodge, Theodore led a group of seventy independents who tried to nominate dull but honest Senator George F. Edmunds of Vermont. Edmunds lost, and lost big, to Blaine.

The defeat didn't surprise Theodore, but it probably added to his discouragement with public life. It appeared that the Old Guard was firmly in charge of the Republican Party, and there was little future for a reform-minded independent. "I have very little expectation of being able to keep on in politics; my success so far has only been won by absolute indifference to my future career," he had stated in an earlier letter to an Albany newspaper. "I will not stay in public life unless I can do so on my own terms, And my ideal, whether lived up to or not, is rather a high one."

At the Chicago convention he told a newspaper reporter simply, "I am going cattle ranching in Dakota. . . . What I shall do after that I cannot tell you."

$$\star \; \star \; 4 \; \star \; \star$$

TWENTY-FOUR HOURS AFTER leaving Chicago, Theodore was in the Dakota Territory, where the only noise was the wind and where a man could ride a horse for days without seeing another person. He hoped being "far off from all mankind" would ease his grief. It seemed to work.

"Having a glorious time here," TR wrote to Bamie. "I have been playing at frontier hunter in good earnest, having been off entirely alone, with my horse and rifle. . . . I felt as absolutely free as a man could feel."

Ranchers, Theodore explained to friends back east, were sort of like Southern plantation owners or Arab sheiks; in other words, they were the frontier's upper class. Even though he had yet to earn any money

Theodore wearing his custom-made cowboy outfit, 1884.

from his ranch, it appeared to be a life that he could commit to. Theodore bought a half dozen horses and another thousand head of cattle. He also bought a second ranch, which he named Chimney Butte, and hired two Maine woodsmen to move west to build him a house overlooking the Little Missouri River.

Out west, just as he did in Albany, Theodore stood out as a dude. The famous Manhattan jeweler Tiffany had made his silver-mounted hunting knife. It matched the silver and gold on his Colt .45 revolver, silver belt buckle, and silver spurs, which were engraved with his initials. And his clothing was still eye-catching, as TR described in one letter: "I wear a sombrero, silk neckerchief, fringed buckskin shirt, sealskin chaparajos or riding trousers; alligator hide boots . . . with my pearl hilted revolver and beautifully finished Winchester rifle, I shall feel able to face anything."

His ranch hands—men with names such as Hashknife Simpson, Bronco Charlie Miller, and Hell-Roaring Jones—called him boss or Mr. Roosevelt. Despite the formality, there was still plenty of kidding. Glasses were seen as a sign of "defective moral character," Theodore wrote. "When I went among strangers I always had to spend twenty-four hours in living down the fact that I wore spectacles."

And of course the boss didn't talk like a cowboy. During one cattle roundup, in his high-pitched voice, Theodore ordered his men to "hasten forward quickly there." And he lacked cowboy skills. He wasn't good at roping, said one cowhand, nor was he "a purty rider."

While the cowboys sometimes laughed at their boss, his energy and hard work impressed them. TR described a typical workday during a cattle roundup in a letter to his friend Cabot Lodge in Massachusetts: "I have been three weeks on the roundup and have worked as hard as any of the cowboys; but I have enjoyed it greatly . . . yesterday I was eighteen hours in the saddle—from 4 A.M. to 10 P.M.—having a half hour each for dinner and tea."

The boss's courage also impressed the cowboys. People on the Dakota plains still tell stories about him. One story is like a scene from a western novel. Theodore walked into a saloon one afternoon and a drunk with a .45 in each hand spotted the well-dressed rancher and shouted, "Four eyes is going to treat." Thinking the man was joking about him buying drinks for everyone, Theodore sat at a table. But the drunk followed him and repeated his command. "Well if I've got to, I've got to," Theodore said, standing up. Then he slugged the guy with a right to the jaw, a quick left, and another right. The man fell, hitting his head on the edge of the bar, which knocked him out cold.

Even more dangerous than a drunk cowboy were the hunting trips. During one hunt, he was tracking a grizzly bear through a dark pine forest when suddenly, "cocking my rifle and stepping quickly forward, I found myself face to face with the great bear, who was less than twenty-five feet off, not eight steps." Because of his poor vision Theodore wasn't a marksman, but this time his aim was good; the first shot hit the bear between the eyes. The grizzly was nine feet tall and weighed twelve hundred pounds. He took the skin and skull back to New York to decorate his new home at Oyster Bay.

While he appeared fearless, years later Theodore admitted it wasn't always so. "There were all kinds of things of which I was afraid at first, ranging from grizzly bears, 'mean horses,' and gunfighters, but by acting as if I was not afraid, I gradually ceased to be afraid."

That first summer Theodore returned to New York twice. He began the winter at his ranch, but after a couple of months of what he described as "the still, merciless, terrible cold that broods over the earth like the shadow of silent death," Theodore hastened back to Manhattan and Bamie's warm home.

He depended on his older sister, who was over thirty and unmarried, to take care of his financial and personal affairs. Bamie had sold his town house and was overseeing the construction of his new house on Long Island. She also took care of Theodore's daughter, whom he called Baby Lee. "I shall call her Lee," he explained, "for there can never be another Alice to me, nor could I have another, not even her own child, bear her name."

Theodore spent the first months of 1885 in Manhattan writing his second book, *Hunting Trips of a Ranchman*, which described his Dakota adventures. He dedicated it to "that keenest of Sportsmen and truest of Friends, my Brother Elliott Roosevelt." After serving as best man at Theodore and Alice's wedding, Elliott had spent two years traveling around Europe, visiting China, and hunting tigers in India.

After receiving his share of his mother's estate, some $62,500, Theodore returned to the Dakota Territory and spent $39,000 for an additional fourteen hundred head of cattle, and furnished his new eight-room house on Chimney Butte Ranch, which, unusual on the frontier, included a library stocked with books by James Fenimore Cooper, Nathaniel Hawthorne, and other favorite writers. He divided his time that summer between Chimney Butte and his newly finished home near Oyster Bay, which he had named Sagamore Hill.

Theodore never lost interest in politics, and he regularly corresponded with his old political friends. In mid-September he went to New York for the Republican state convention and ended up staying much longer than he had anticipated.

The pages in Theodore's journal that autumn were often blank except for the letter "E." The E was for Edith Carow. Bamie apparently had arranged an "accidental" meeting between the two. Edith, who was three years younger, had a roundish figure, blue eyes, and peachlike skin. He liked her "sweet manner," and "air of softness and shyness." TR told his younger sister,

Corinne, "You have no idea how sweet Edith is. I don't think even I had known how wonderfully good and unselfish she was."

But his sisters knew Edith quite well because she had been Corinne's best friend when they were children and a frequent visitor to the Roosevelt home. Edith came from an old New York family. They had been well-to-do, but her alcoholic father had squandered most of the money. "Edith we have always known intimately. She is very bright & attractive & I believe absolutely devoted to Theodore," Bamie reported to a friend. The sisters also knew that their brother and Edith were close as teenagers, but some unexplained quarrel had ended a budding romance. Edith was a deeply private person and told Theodore to destroy all of her letters, so little is known about their courtship.

She must have been impressed, as others were, by how her old friend had matured since going west. Theodore was no longer a skinny, awkward-looking youth. Ranch work had made him more muscular, with a thick neck and broad chest and shoulders. Even his voice, at least when he wasn't excited, was deeper. What immediately stood out on Theodore's square, somewhat plump face were his large, blue eyes full of happiness and his big smile with even, pearly-white teeth that appeared to glitter.

In November the couple became secretly engaged. Although he was in love with Edith, Theodore felt he was betraying Alice. "I utterly disbelieve in and disapprove of second marriages," he explained to Bamie. "You could not reproach me one half as bitterly for my inconstancy and unfaithfulness, as I reproach myself." To avoid the publicity of a New York society wedding, the couple decided to marry in England at the end 1886. Early that year Edith accompanied her sister and mother on a long trip abroad while Theodore went west for his last roundup and another frontier adventure.

He returned in March to Chimney Butte, where it was still winter. Soon after his arrival thieves stole one of the ranch's boats. Theodore and two ranch hands pursued the crooks in another boat down the icy Little Missouri River. Two days later they surprised the three thieves who, despite being heavily armed, surrendered without a fight. No one locally would have blamed Theodore for using frontier justice—either shooting or hanging the trio. But he told his men to take the two boats back to Chimney Butte, while he hired a rancher with a wagon to carry the thieves to the nearest jail, which was about forty miles away in Dickinson. Armed with a pistol and rifle, Theodore walked the entire way behind the wagon since the three prisoners weren't tied up and he didn't trust the rancher. At night, he stayed awake by the fire reading Tolstoy's *Anna Karenina*. After finishing that book, Theodore borrowed a paperback novel from one of his prisoners about the outlaw Jesse James. By the time the men reached Dickinson, Theodore's feet were badly blistered, and, after turning his prisoners over to the sheriff, he immediately saw a doctor.

This and other episodes during the short time Theodore lived in the Dakota Territory made a big impression on westerners, as expressed by an editorial in the *Sioux Falls Press*. "He is one of the finest thoroughbreds you ever met—a whole souled, clear headed, high minded gentleman. When he first was on the range, the cowboys took him for a dude, but soon they realized the stuff of which the youngster was built, and there is no man who now inspires such enthusiastic regard among them as he."

Later in his life, Theodore would exaggerate the amount of time he spent out west, claiming it was the "major part of seven years." Actually, it was only about a year all together, but it was a significant year. A biographer called it "one of the great formative experiences of his life."

Back in New York City the Republicans persuaded Theodore to run for mayor in the November elections, even though there was little hope he would win in the three-way race between Republicans, Democrats, and a new political power called the United Labor Party. Theodore ran an energetic campaign but still came in third behind Henry George, the United Labor Party candidate who barely lost to the Democrat. Soon afterward Theodore and Bamie sailed to England, where he would marry Edith.

★ ★ 5 ★ ★

AFTER A FIFTEEN-WEEK honeymoon in Europe, Edith and Theodore moved into Sagamore Hill, which was about a mile from the Long Island village of Oyster Bay and some thirty miles east of New York City. It was a special place, as he later explained, where "we love a great many things—birds and trees and books, and all things beautiful, and horses and rifles and children and hard work and the joy of life."

The three-story house sat on a hill overlooking Long Island Sound and 150 acres of fields. Its twenty-two-rooms, heated by two furnaces and eight fireplaces, included a parlor, a library, and—not counting servants' quarters—ten bedrooms. The couple filled their home with oak and leather furniture. On the walls they hung Theodore's hunting trophies, glass-eyed heads of elk and deer, and on the hardwood floors they spread thick buffalo skins and bear skins.

Edith had a study on the first floor where she could read her favorite authors: Shakespeare, Trollope, Milton, and Shelley. And since she was much better than her husband at managing money and keeping records, Edith managed Sagamore Hill's expenses as well as its servants and gardeners.

Theodore's study, which he called the Gun Room, was on the third floor. As the name suggests, he kept his guns there, as well as photographs of his ranches and stacks of books by Sir Walter Scott, Henry Wadsworth Longfellow, and dozens of other writers. On one wall hung two small portraits of the Civil War leaders who had saved the Union: Abraham Lincoln and Ulysses S. Grant. Hanging between them was a large portrait of his father.

At first, Theodore had planned to leave his daughter with Bamie, where she had been all three years of her life. "If you wish to," he had informed his older sister, "you shall keep Baby Lee, I of course paying the expense." But Edith put her foot down, saying the child was now her daughter, too, and should live with them.

Theodore, Edith, and their growing family at Sagamore Hill, 1894.

And soon there were two children at Sagamore Hill.

Edith gave birth September 13, 1887, to Theodore Roosevelt Jr., whom the family called Ted. "The boy is a fine little fellow about 8 1/2 pounds," Theodore wrote. "I am very glad our house has an heir at last!" He enjoyed being a father. His daughter was "too sweet and good . . . as for Ted, he crawls everywhere . . . and is too merry and happy for anything. I go in to play with them every morning; they are certainly the dearest children imaginable."

Theodore spent part of the summer with Elliott

fox hunting and playing polo. His younger brother had rented an estate fifteen miles away in Hempstead. Three and a half years earlier, Elliott had married an attractive debutant named Anna Hall, in what a New York newspaper called "one of the most brilliant social events of the season." The couple had one child, Eleanor. Theodore and his sisters, both of whom were living in Manhattan, had hoped the responsibilities of a family would make their brother settle down. But that didn't happen. Years later Edith would bluntly describe Elliott as a man who "drank like a fish and ran after the ladies."

With his inheritance practically gone, Theodore worked hard to earn a living as a "literary feller." He appeared to be devoting himself to writing. "I shall probably never be in politics again," he informed an old Republican friend. "My literary work occupies a good deal of my time; and I have on the whole done fairly well at it."

His first book, *The Naval War of 1812*, had earned praise but not money. More successful was his second book, *Hunting Trips of a Ranchman*, and two companion books about his experiences in the Dakota Territory, which a reviewer praised as "tinglingly alive, masculine and vascular."

Thanks to his Massachusetts friend Cabot Lodge, who also wrote books on American history, the Boston-based publisher Houghton Mifflin had given Theodore contracts to write biographies of two American statesmen. He had finished the first biography in 1886, and it was published in 1887. It was about Thomas Hart Benton. Theodore identified with Benton, a wealthy easterner who early in the nineteenth century moved to the Mississippi River Valley, which at the time was the American frontier. Benton later became a U.S. senator from Missouri. He was a combative politician who firmly believed in Manifest Destiny, the popular nineteenth-century idea that the United States should expand westward all the way to the Pacific Ocean.

Shortly after settling into Sagamore Hill, Theodore began work on his second biography, about a lesser-known Founding Father with the unusual name of Gouverneur Morris. Again, as a Roosevelt biographer has noted, there were striking similarities between author and subject. They were well-born New Yorkers, literate and widely traveled. Both were aggressive moralists and passionate patriots who believed in a strong federal government.

Theodore complained that "writing is horribly hard work for me; and I make slow progress," but using a steel nib pen that required frequent dipping into an ink well, he finished his 92,000-word manuscript on Morris (a typed, double-spaced manuscript of that length would be about 350 pages) in just three months.

After finishing that biography Theodore decided that he wanted to "write some book that would really take rank as in the very first class." It was a dream the author planned to pursue by writing *The Winning of the West*, a multivolume history about the exploration and settlement of America. Theodore started work in early 1888, assuring his editor at Putnam that he would deliver the first two volumes within a year. But rather than getting to work immediately, as any writer who had to deliver two books in twelve months should have done, he decided to go west to hunt and check on his cattle herd.

The men who managed his ranch had already written that the previous winter had been the worst anyone could remember and many of his cattle had frozen or starved to death. Theodore found that he had lost two-thirds of his herd. It was a big financial blow. He had invested $85,000 in his cattle business, and there was no chance of earning any of that investment back.

Theodore was equally disturbed by what he saw, or didn't see, while hunting; the once abundant wildlife had all but vanished. The growing number of white people moving into the region, "swinish butchers" he called them, had not only killed most of the buffalo, but they had also killed most of the elk, grizzly, and other wildlife. And overgrazing had stripped away so much grass that the prairie had begun to look like desert.

The destruction led Theodore to found one of the first organizations in the country devoted to conserving natural resources. Back in New York, he organized the Boone and Crockett Club, which was named for two of America's most famous frontiersmen, Daniel Boone and Davy Crockett. Theodore was the club's first president, and he recruited other members who were prominent scientists, lawyers, and politicians.

They persuaded the federal government to do more to protect Yellowstone National Park in Wyoming, the nation's first national park, from destructive tourists. And they lobbied Congress to pass the Forest Reserve Act, a law giving the U.S. president the authority to remove large tracts of forests from the public domain and place them under federal supervision. This was the beginning of the National Forest Service.

That fall Theodore once again changed his mind about getting involved in politics and campaigned for Republican Benjamin Harrison, who was running against the incumbent Democratic president, Grover Cleveland. Harrison was a former Indiana senator and the grandson of the ninth president, William Henry Harrison, who, after serving only thirty-one days, had the distinction of being the first American president to die in office. Theodore campaigned in Illinois, Michigan, and Minnesota, where his fiery take-no-prisoners style established him as one of his party's most popular speakers. Harrison won the presidency, and Republicans won majorities in both the House and the Senate.

When President Harrison took office in March 1889, Theodore asked his friend Lodge, who was now a congressman, and his wife, Nannie, to try to get him appointed assistant secretary of state. The best jobs went to the party's biggest donors, so Theodore didn't expect a major appointment. He was probably overreaching by asking for the job of assistant secretary.

The new secretary of state, James G. Blaine, told Nannie Lodge, only half jokingly, that having Roosevelt in command of the nation's foreign policy would ruin his vacations. "I do fear somehow that my sleep would not be quite as easy and refreshing if so brilliant and aggressive a man had hold of the helm. Matters are constantly occurring which require the most thoughtful concentration and the most stubborn inaction. Do you think that Mr. T.R.'s temperament would give guaranty of that course?" Anyone who knew Theodore knew the answer to that question. The president ended up offering him a different job.

★ ★ 6 ★ ★

PRESIDENT HARRISON HAD been wary of giving Roosevelt any job—and for good reason it would turn out—but he decided to appoint him civil service commissioner.

The bipartisan Civil Service Commission was in charge of enforcing the Pendleton Act, which had been passed only six years earlier in 1883. Each time the White House changed parties the new president's political appointees fired thousands of federal workers and replaced them with people who often had no qualifications other than having voted for the winner. Harrison's attorney general described the qualifications needed by federal job seekers. He must be "first a good man, second a good Republican." The Pendleton Act

TR in his Sagamore Hill library, 1895.

protected about one-fifth of the 159,356 federal jobs in 1889 from political meddling. It also established the civil service exam, which employees had to pass to qualify for the protected jobs. And it prohibited the common practice of forcing government employees to contribute money to specific candidates.

Being civil service commissioner would mean fights with Old Guard Republicans, and Theodore's friends were afraid it would ruin his political future, but he seemed unconcerned. "I am a great believer in practical politics," the new commissioner insisted, "but when my duty is to enforce a law, that law is surely going to be enforced, without fear or favor . . . while I'm in I mean business."

In May, Commissioner Roosevelt left his family at Sagamore Hill and went to Washington to begin his first federal job. There were two other commissioners, a Democrat and a Republican. They both were older, but they let the younger man have the largest office and take the lead.

Soon after settling into his new position Theodore saw trouble ahead. John Wanamaker, a rich department-store owner from Philadelphia, Pennsylvania, had helped raise the then-incredible sum of $4 million to elect Harrison. As a reward, the new president appointed him postmaster general, the official in charge of every post office in all thirty-eight states in the Union. The U.S. Postal Service was the largest federal agency and employed over half of all federal employees. In only six weeks on the job, Wanamaker had turned the service upside down by replacing nearly one-third of all postal workers—some thirty thousand people.

There was a lot of wrongdoing to investigate, but Commissioner Roosevelt wanted cases that would make newspaper headlines and promote the commission's work, as well as his own career. He first traveled to Indianapolis, Indiana, President Harrison's hometown, to investigate postal service hiring practices there. People in that city had complained that the president's close friend, Postmaster William Wallace, had violated civil service laws by hiring three men who had been fired from previous postal jobs for taking bribes. In the Indiana capital, Theodore held a hearing on the allegations and determined they were true. The postmaster had no choice but to obey the law and dismiss the three men. The incident attracted newspaper attention to Roosevelt's efforts to enforce civil service laws and, as he expected, drew howls of protest from Old Guard Republicans.

Back in Washington, in early October 1889 Theodore received a telegram that his second son had been born several weeks prematurely. He took a train to New York City, but missed the last scheduled train to Long Island. Heedless of the expense, Theodore chartered a train to rush him to Oyster Bay. Arriving at Sagamore Hill at four A.M. he found Edith and the new baby, who was named Kermit for one of Edith's relatives, doing well under Bamie's care.

More good news that year, including the publication of the first two volumes of *Winning the West*, which Theodore had completed on schedule. The books received good reviews, and he planned on writing two more volumes of *Winning the West* as well as a history of New York City.

Just before Christmas that year, Edith decided that she and the children should move to Washington. "Alice needs someone to laugh and romp with her instead of a sober and staid person like me," she told her husband. The family rented a row house one-tenth the size of their Sagamore Hill home. With three children and two homes to support, money was a bigger problem than ever. Edith, as always, handled the finances. Just paying the rent, the servants, and the grocery bills took all of her husband's annual $3,500 salary. Edith, cutting back as much as possible, saved money by grinding up fish bones to make tooth powder and giving her husband an allowance, which he always seemed to spend without knowing where.

While Edith spent much of 1890 worried about paying the bills and Theodore wondered how long he'd keep his job as commissioner, they faced another, larger problem. TR called it a "nightmare of horror." In December, Anna Roosevelt telegrammed from Vienna, Austria, that she was pregnant and that Theodore's younger brother Elliott was drinking heavily. She was afraid he would harm her or their five-year-old daughter Eleanor or one-year-old Elliott Jr. Anna wanted Bamie to come to Vienna to get Elliott to stop drinking. Bamie agreed, but before her scheduled trip in February there was more trouble.

A lawyer for one of Anna and Elliott's former maids, a young woman named Katy Mann, sent

Commissioner Roosevelt a letter advising him that she was pregnant with Elliott's baby and that she expected financial assistance. Elliott denied being the father in his letters, but asked his brother to give Katy money anyway. Theodore insisted she was lying and vowed never to pay her a dime. Despite this resolve, he worried about the scandal. "It is horrible, awful; it is like a brooding nightmare. If it was mere death one could stand it; it is the shame that is so fearful."

After Bamie arrived in Europe, she reported that Elliott had taken his family to Paris, where he was constantly drunk and going about the city with a mistress. Plus, Elliott was being abusive toward Anna and threatened to cut off all support if she left him.

As Theodore waited for more news from Bamie through the spring of 1891, the showdown with John Wanamaker began to unfold. A lawyer informed Theodore that the postmaster in Baltimore, Maryland, had violated civil service law. The postmaster was a Harrison appointee, and had been collecting $5 to $10 "contributions" from his employees to support pro-Harrison candidates in an upcoming Republican primary. Commissioner Roosevelt forwarded the lawyer's accusations to Wanamaker, suggesting that he investigate. But the postmaster general did nothing.

On primary day, Theodore went to Baltimore and witnessed post office employees buying votes and bribing election officials. He talked to these employees, who made no effort to hide what they were doing. An office holder's duty, Commissioner Roosevelt later admonished, "is to do the work of the Government for the whole people, and not to pervert his office for the use of any party or any faction."

The commissioner recommended firing twenty-five Baltimore postal employees, but when the story appeared in the newspaper, Old Guard Republicans insisted it was the commissioner who should be fired. President Harrison, mindful that a growing number of progressive voters favored civil service reform, said he wouldn't do anything until he saw a report. Theodore waited until the following summer, when much of official Washington was on vacation, before sending copies of his 146-page report to the postmaster general's office and the president.

Meanwhile, it was a summer for new Roosevelts. Anna gave birth to her second son, Gracie Hall

Roosevelt; Edith gave birth to her first daughter, Ethel Roosevelt; and Katy Mann gave birth to Elliott Roosevelt Mann.

Soon afterward Katy offered to drop her lawsuit for $10,000, but Theodore felt that the sum—more than three times his annual salary—was outrageous. Even though a "likeness expert" said the boy definitely looked like a Roosevelt, Theodore prepared to fight her claim in court and warned his uncles and cousins to brace themselves for unpleasant publicity. But by autumn the scandal had faded, suggesting that somebody did pay Katy, but the details remain a family secret.

Meanwhile, Theodore and Bamie asked the court to declare Elliot legally insane to prevent him from squandering his inheritance. The press got wind of the story and made it front-page news: "Elliott Roosevelt Insane: His Brother Theodore Applies for a Writ in Lunacy." Theodore knew the court would take several months to reach a decision, and he was afraid details about the case would become public. "What a hideous tale of his life we should have to testify to if put on the stand," he told Bamie. Taking time off from work to "settle the thing once for all," Theodore traveled to Paris in January 1892, where, much to his surprise and relief, Elliot readily agreed to return home and be treated for his alcoholism. Anna and the children would move to New York.

Back in Washington, Theodore learned that Wanamaker's staff had conducted its own investigation of the Baltimore post office. But the postmaster general refused to let anyone see the nine-hundred-plus-page report. There was little Commissioner Roosevelt could do but complain about the "hypocritical haberdasher!"

Nearly a year after the Maryland primary, Theodore took his report on the Baltimore post office to the Congressional Civil Service Reform Committee, which was chaired by a Democrat who was happy to hold a hearing. Wanamaker told the committee that his investigation found that Commissioner Roosevelt had frightened and badgered the postal employees into confessing things they weren't doing. And that the workers had been soliciting funds only to buy a pool table to use on breaks.

The committee asked to see the postmaster general's report, and it turned out that Wanamaker's investigators had found as much wrongdoing as Theodore had. But Wanamaker had ignored civil service laws and then lied about it. "The exposure he has suffered from Mr. Roosevelt is merciless and humiliating," commented *The New York Times,* "but it is clearly deserved." Nothing happened to Wanamaker other than a stain on his reputation as a public-service-minded, church-going citizen. And he went on to be involved in several other scandals during his four-year term.

The Wanamaker scandals, high tariffs on imports, and the growing anger in the Midwest at the government's failure to regulate big business contributed to President Harrison's defeat in the 1892 election. Voters reelected Democrat Grover Cleveland, the incumbent who had been ousted four years earlier. Cleveland is the only president to have served two separate terms.

Theodore wanted to stay in Washington and he urged his friends to persuade the new president to re-appoint him as civil service commissioner. Cleveland knew that Theodore, despite his small staff and budget, had achieved a lot in four years. He had made civil service more democratic by opening more government jobs for women. And he changed civil service exams to make sure applicants were tested for skills needed in their jobs. For example, the commissioner didn't think border patrolmen necessarily needed to know how to read or write. It was more important that they were able to ride a horse and shoot a gun. So part of the new test took place on a firing range. (This change prompted a friend to suggest that the commissioner could find the best border guards by having candidates shoot at each other and then hiring the survivors.)

An editorial in the *Philadelphia Record* described TR's role as commissioner: "His colleagues were quiet men, who supported him to a considerable extent, but he did the fighting in the newspapers, before Congress and everywhere else . . . he became recognized as the leading spirit of the Commission." Sixty-two years later, one of the commission's chairmen said that stories of Theodore's accomplishments "are handed down from generation to generation of Commission employees."

Theodore accepted President Cleveland's invitation to remain at the commission, but once again he was preoccupied with family problems when twenty-nine-year-old Anna Roosevelt died of diphtheria.

Anna's mother took custody of the three children, but the following May four-year-old Elliott Jr. also died of diphtheria. His father, who had been sober for four years, began drinking again. "Elliott has sunk to the lowest depths," Edith wrote to her mother. He "consorts with the vilest women." Theodore and his sisters received "horrid anonymous letters about his life," she wrote. "I live in constant dread of some scandal of his attaching itself to Theodore."

For his part, Theodore ignored his brother and wanted his younger sister to do the same. "I do wish Corinne could get a little of my hard heart about Elliott," he complained to Bamie. "She can do, and ought to do, nothing for him. He can't be helped, and he must simply be let go his own gait." But their brother soon ceased to be a problem.

In August 1894, in a fit of delirium tremens, which is hallucinations and disorientation experienced by some chronic alcoholics, Elliott had a convulsion and died in the Manhattan apartment where he lived with his mistress. Theodore was "more overcome than I have ever seen him," Corinne wrote, and he "cried like a child for a long time."

By that time Theodore wanted to move back to New York. After six years in Washington, he felt he needed to reestablish himself in the Republican Party in his home state. He said years later that it was during his time as civil service commissioner that he first started thinking about being president. "I used to walk past the White House, and my heart would beat a little faster as the thought came to me that possibly— possibly—I would some day occupy it as President." Being mayor of New York City or governor of New York State was a good stepping-stone to the presidency.

The Republicans had asked Theodore to run for mayor of New York in 1894, but Edith was dead set against the idea. She had given birth the previous April to her fourth child, Archie. The worst recession in the nation's history had begun that year, and she worried that Theodore might lose the election, leaving them with five children and no income. The Roosevelts were already having so much financial trouble that they considered selling Sagamore Hill.

An opportunity to move back to Sagamore Hill, as well as double his salary, came in 1895 when New York's new mayor William Strong offered Theodore a

$6,000-a-year job as one of the city's four police commissioners. The mayor, a businessman with no political experience, had won the election by promising to clean up corruption in city government. The police department was especially corrupt, and Theodore knew the job would be difficult. But he accepted it, telling Bamie, "I must make up my mind to much criticism and disappointment."

As usual, Theodore soon got the attention of local journalists. "We have a real Police Commissioner," wrote one in the *New York World*. "His teeth are big and white, his eyes are small and piercing, his voice is rasping . . . he looks like a man of strength . . . a determined man, a fighting man, an honest, conscientious man." Another article praised Theodore because "he has great qualities which make him an invaluable public servant—inflexible honesty, absolute fearlessness, and devotion to good government which amounts to religion."

Despite the initial fanfare, the job proved frustrating and ultimately impossible. Theodore's three colleagues had made him president of the commission, but personality and political differences soon made them uncooperative. And he lost public support when he began enforcing the law that prohibited saloons from opening on Sundays.

Over three-quarters of New York City's population was foreign-born. Many of these immigrants enjoyed spending Sundays, often their only day off, at neighborhood saloons with beer and friends. Theodore said he had to choose between "closing all of the saloons and violating my oath of office." But the public protest was so loud that even Mayor Strong began ridiculing the commissioner's efforts. Being police commissioner was the most frustrating job Theodore would ever hold, so he was glad for the opportunity to take time off in 1896 to campaign for former Ohio governor William McKinley, who was running for president.

Theodore called that election the biggest crisis the nation had faced since 1861. It was an exaggeration, but it did express how Republicans felt about a third party gathering strength in the Midwest and South.

Third parties rarely do well in American politics, but the Populist Party was more successful than most. It was organized by small farm owners, tenant farmers, and sharecroppers who felt excluded from the two established political parties and exploited by the railroads, banks, and other big businesses. They wanted, among other things, the government to take over the railroads and banks. And they wanted U.S. senators to be elected directly by the people rather than appointed by conservative state legislatures. In 1896, the Democrats and the Populists joined in an uneasy alliance to back the Democratic presidential candidate William Jennings Bryan, a handsome thirty-six-year-old lawyer whose gift for public speaking drew huge crowds. The Democrats and Populists had lots of enthusiasm, but little money. They raised only about $300,000 for Bryan's presidential campaign.

That's about how much money Standard Oil alone gave to the Republican candidate, who collected a total of $7 million for his campaign. While farmers in the Midwest paraded for Bryan, stockbrokers and bankers in New York paraded for McKinley.

Theodore plunged into battle, ridiculing farmers and other rural Populists: "A taste for learning and cultivated friends, and a tendency to bathe frequently, cause them the deepest suspicion." Theodore was equally caustic about the Democratic candidate. "Instead of government of the people, for the people, and by the people, which we now have, Bryan would substitute a government of the mob." McKinley comfortably won the election by about six hundred thousand votes.

"You may easily imagine our relief over the election," TR wrote to Bamie. "It was the greatest crisis in our national fate, save only the Civil War. And I am more than glad I was able to do my part in the contest." McKinley rewarded his star campaigner with a new job, and Theodore returned to Washington to set in motion the events that would make him a national hero.

$\star \ \star \ 7 \ \star \ \star$

"TO PREPARE FOR war is the most effectual means to promote peace," Theodore quoted one of his favorite presidents, George Washington, in a June 2 speech at the Naval War College in Newport, Rhode Island. It was his first major speech since he had started his new job as assistant secretary of the navy on April 19, 1897. He kept the job for only one year. Yet those dozen months were momentous for both the man and the nation.

While Assistant Secretary Roosevelt was a relatively minor figure in Washington, he had big objectives. The United States had the world's fifth-largest navy, but he wanted to make it bigger. "We need a large Navy," he said, "a full proportion of powerful battleships able to meet those of any other nation."

A strong navy would also help accomplish other

goals. President McKinley, like previous presidents, was reluctant to get involved in the affairs of other nations, but Theodore wanted the United States to exert its influence beyond its own borders, especially on neighboring countries. "I hope to see the Spanish flag and the English flag gone from the map of North America before I'm sixty," he stated. It was unlikely that the United States could chase Great Britain out of Canada any time soon, but Spain was another matter. The Spanish, who once had one of the world's largest colonial empires, now possessed only a group of far-flung islands. The most significant of these islands were Cuba in the Caribbean and the Philippines in the Pacific Ocean.

Theodore had his eye on Cuba, just ninety miles south of Key West, Florida, where *insurrectos*, or rebels, were fighting for a *Cuba libre*. Cubans had been trying to win independence from Spain for decades. The latest fighting began in 1895, and U.S. newspapers covered it closely. One reason they paid close attention was that the Cuban rebels kept an office in New York City and fed stories to the press. Plus, stories and photographs about the conflict sold newspapers. The public didn't mind reading about the bloody rebellion, but most people felt the United States shouldn't get involved. Not Theodore.

"We ought to drive the Spaniards out of Cuba," TR wrote to his older sister. "It would be a good thing, in more ways than one." The assistant secretary, who worked at a Civil War–era wooden desk with an American flag carved in the front and carved cannons protruding from the sides, did his best to make that happen.

He began by collecting a group of people who shared his interest in expanding America's influence abroad. These like-minded and influential individuals included Cabot Lodge, who had been appointed to the Senate three years earlier. (Senators were not directly elected by voters until 1914.) The group also included Commodore George Dewey, one of the navy's highest ranking officers; William H. Taft, a federal judge; and Captain Leonard Wood, an army doctor and President McKinley's personal physician. These men and others often got together over lunch at Washington's exclusive Metropolitan Club to talk about foreign policy.

In the summer of 1897 Theodore urged his boss, Secretary John D. Long, who was nearly sixty, to take a long vacation. In early August, he did just that, going to his Massachusetts home for two months. "The secretary is away," Theodore told a friend, "and I'm having immense fun running the Navy." And just two weeks later, the *New York Sun* reported, "The decks are cleared for action. Acting Secretary Roosevelt . . . has the whole navy bordering on a war footing."

"I did not hesitate to take responsibilities," the assistant secretary recalled. "I have continually meddled with what was not my business." Even when Secretary Long returned from his vacation, Theodore continued to meddle. One day, while his boss was out of the office, Theodore read a letter addressed to Long. It was from a senator recommending that Commodore John A. Howell be given command of the navy's fleet of warships in the Pacific Ocean. Theodore thought his friend Commodore Dewey would be a better commander, especially if there was war with Spain.

Theodore called Dewey and told him to quickly send one of his friends in Congress to speak to the president. A few hours later, Senator Redfield Proctor of Vermont called on President McKinley. Unaware that another naval officer had been recommended for the position, McKinley sent a letter to Secretary Long asking him to give Dewey the job. The secretary had to agree to the president's "request."

That fall, in time for Theodore's thirty-ninth birthday, Edith and the children moved to Washington. The family had barely settled into their home when, on November 19, Edith gave birth to her fifth child, Quentin. The newborn, just as his three brothers had been, was immediately put on the waiting list for admission to the exclusive Groton School, a boys' boarding school in Massachusetts.

Edith was slow to recover from Quentin's birth. No doubt remembering his first wife's fate during childbirth fourteen years earlier, Theodore consulted several doctors. One said Edith had an abscess near her hip and might die if she didn't have an operation. But surgery at that time was primitive and dangerous, so Theodore was hesitant about following the doctor's advice.

Ten-year-old Ted was also a concern. He had frequent headaches and was withdrawn, which was not normal for a Roosevelt. The doctor said the boy was overwrought from trying to live up to his father's expectations. Theodore wanted his children to be tough, and he tended to push them even when playing. He was, his oldest daughter recalled, "the instigator of all those perfectly awful endurance tests masquerading as games!"

Theodore made no secret of what he expected. "I want my boys trained to be hardy, self-reliant, positive men . . . rather than see them grow up namby-pamby weaklings I would rather see them put to death." He especially pushed Ted, his namesake, because the boy had the potential "to be all the things I would like to have been and wasn't, and it has been a great temptation to push him." But the doctor's diagnosis made Theodore vow to "never press Ted in body or mind," which he didn't for a while.

As Theodore worried about Edith and Ted, early in 1898 riots broke out in Havana, Cuba's capital and largest city. The president sent the battleship USS *Maine* to protect American citizens and businesses there. On February 15, while the *Maine* was anchored in Havana's harbor, an explosion sank the battleship and killed 262 American sailors. No one knew who or what caused the explosion, but Theodore called it "an act of dirty treachery on the part of the Spaniards."

Because of the *Maine* disaster, war fever spread

across the country. Newspapers published hundreds of stories, many of them exaggerated or completely untrue, about Spanish atrocities in Cuba. "Blood on the roadsides, blood in the fields, blood on the doorsteps, blood, blood, blood! The old, the young, the weak, the crippled—are all butchered without mercy," screamed a typical article in Joseph Pulitzer's *New York World*. Such stories, called "yellow journalism," sold lots of newspapers while inflaming public anger. "To Hell with Spain! Remember the *Maine!*" was a popular expression summing up the public's mood.

Meanwhile, Assistant Secretary Roosevelt continued to meddle. Before leaving his office one February afternoon, Secretary Long, well aware by now that his assistant had no qualms about making major decisions on his own, told him not to do anything that would affect "the policy of the administration without consulting the President or me." After Long left, the assistant secretary telegrammed Commodore Dewey, who was now in Hong Kong with the Pacific fleet, to prepare for "offensive operations in the Philippines." He also ordered large supplies of ammunition and guns. Then he sent messages to Congress asking for legislation to recruit thousands of new sailors. In a single afternoon, one historian observed, the assistant secretary had the navy more prepared for combat than at any time since the Civil War.

"During my short absence," Secretary Long marveled the next day, "I find that Roosevelt, in his precipitate way, has come very near causing more of an explosion than happened to the *Maine* . . . the very devil seemed to possess him yesterday afternoon." Although angry, Long didn't change the orders. He knew that his assistant secretary was quite knowledgeable about naval affairs and his decisions were usually right, regardless of how impulsive they seemed.

Elsewhere in the nation, people debated the pros and cons of a war. The United States was just recovering from a major economic recession, which was called the Panic of 1893. Big business, which had contributed record amounts of money to elect McKinley in 1896, initially opposed a war because it might slow economic recovery. But as the public clamor to avenge the *Maine* grew louder, Wall Street joined in. Spain hadn't been a major military power for centuries, and its warships were old, so the United States would certainly win without too many casualties. And Republican politicians felt that a successful war would help their candidates in congressional elections that fall and in the 1900 presidential election.

On April 11, the president, as specified in the Constitution, asked Congress for a declaration of war. The legislators debated for eight days. On the morning of April 19, 1898, exactly one year after Theodore had become assistant secretary, both the House and the Senate voted to declare war on Spain.

President McKinley ordered Dewey to attack Spanish warships at Manila, Spain's colonial capital of the Philippines. In the Battle of Manila Bay on May 1, 1898, in just a few hours the American navy destroyed all eleven enemy ships, killing some 150 Spanish sailors while losing only one man, from heat stroke.

Theodore resigned as assistant secretary on May 16 because he wanted to go to war himself. "If I am to be any use in politics it is because I am supposed to be a man who does not preach what he fears to practice. . . . For the last year I have preached war with Spain. I would feel distinctly ashamed . . . if I now failed to practice what I have preached." Or, as he said on another occasion, "I have a horror of people who bark but don't bite."

Friends and family tried to convince Theodore that at age thirty-nine he was too old to be a soldier. His eyesight wasn't good enough, he had no military training, and he had six children to consider. Twice, the president asked Theodore to stay in Washington to help manage war operations. He "has lost his head," Secretary Long wrote in his diary. "He thinks he is following his highest ideal, whereas, in fact, as without exception every one of his friends advises him, he is acting like a fool."

Edith, who had nearly died after finally having her operation in early March, did not want her husband to go to war either, but she knew she couldn't stop him. "I know now," Theodore said later, "that I should have turned from my wife's deathbed" to fight in Cuba.

As adults, both Alice and her cousin Corinney said they thought Theodore had been embarrassed because his father hadn't served in the Civil War. "He felt," Corinney commented, "he had to explain it always, about the father he admired so hugely."

Secretary of War Russell A. Alger gave Theodore

an army commission as a lieutenant colonel and gave him permission to recruit his own regiment of cowboys from out west. It had been common during the Civil War for prominent men to recruit and command their own regiments. And several men in addition to Theodore recruited regiments for the Spanish-American War. Colonel Roosevelt had no military training and he wisely suggested that he serve as second in command under his friend, career soldier Leonard Wood, who had been promoted to full colonel. But everyone, Colonel Wood included, knew who was really in charge.

News that Colonel Roosevelt was looking for men spread quickly, and he received 23,000 applications. The colonel, using no particular method, personally chose 780 men from the West and later added about 200 men from the East and South. Theodore said the 1st United States Volunteer Cavalry Regiment was "as typical an American regiment as ever marched or fought. We have a few from everywhere including a score of Indians and about as many men of Mexican origin from New Mexico; then there are some fifty Easterners—almost all graduates of Harvard, Yale,

Princeton, etc.—and almost as many Southerners. Three fourths of our men have at one time or another been cowboys or else are small stockmen."

Newspapermen, as always, were drawn to Theodore. The reporters tried various alliterative names for the regiment—Teddy's Terrors, Roosevelt's Rangers, Cavalry Cowpunchers, Teddy's Texas Tarantulas, Teddy's Righteous Rounders—before finding one they liked, Roosevelt's Rough Riders.

Theodore, true to his reputation as a dude, ordered a tailor-made uniform from Brooks Brothers in New York, and he had the foresight to sew twelve pairs of glasses into the lining of his hat. His men wore a distinctive uniform of blue flannel shirts, brown trousers, slouch hats, leggings, boots, and blue bandannas knotted around the neck.

After training several weeks in San Antonio, Texas, the Rough Riders rode by train to Tampa, Florida, where they joined thousands of other soldiers squeezing onto a flotilla of ships bound for Cuba. The expedition was led by General William Rufus Shafter, a three-hundred-pound veteran of the Civil War. Theodore criticized General Shafter from the beginning. "The folly, the lack of preparation, are almost inconceivable," he noted in his journal. There weren't enough vessels, so over half of the Rough Riders and all of the regiment's horses, except those for officers, had to be left behind. Nonetheless, the sixteen thousand soldiers and three thousand horses and mules that embarked on June 14, 1898, were, at that time, the largest American military expedition ever sent abroad.

Eight days later the Americans waded ashore in Cuba and fought their first battle. "Yesterday we struck the Spaniards and had a brisk fight for 2 ½ hours," Theodore wrote to Corinne. "We lost a dozen men killed or mortally wounded, and sixty severely or slightly wounded. One man was killed as he stood beside a tree with me. . . . The last charge I led on the left using a rifle I took from a wounded man. . . . The fire was very hot at one or two points where the men around me went down like ninepins." After the battle he picked up bullet casings as souvenirs for his children.

The "fight really was a capital thing for me," Colonel Roosevelt felt, "for practically all the men had served under my actual command, and thenceforth felt enthusiastic belief that I would lead them alright." The colonel, even though he had a horse, chose to march with his men on the rough road to the port city of Santiago, in southeastern Cuba. The Americans were attacking that city because six Spanish warships, the only ones in Cuba, huddled in a narrow harbor protected from the American navy by Santiago's batteries.

Colonel Roosevelt, always looking for good publicity, made sure two of his favorite reporters were by his side: Richard Harding Davis of the *New York Herald* and Edward Marshall, who would be paralyzed by a bullet, of the *New York Journal*. Numerous other reporters, including Stephen Crane, the author of *The Red Badge of Courage*, also accompanied the invasion force.

Early on the morning of July 1, American soldiers and Cuban *insurrectos* began their assault on the village of El Caney, just outside Santiago, and on San Juan Heights, the fortified hills protecting the city. The tallest part of the Heights was San Juan Hill. There was a smaller hill nearby that the soldiers called Kettle Hill because of a sugar-refining kettle at the top. At the crests of both hills hundreds of Spanish soldiers, armed with Geman-made Mauser rifles, were

OVERLEAF: Colonel Roosevelt and his men in Cuba, 1897.

entrenched behind barbed wire. Some ten thousand Spanish soldiers were in Santiago. Because several top officers were ill with malaria and dysentery, Colonel Wood was promoted to general and given another command. Theodore was officially in charge of the Rough Riders.

"It was a very lovely morning," he later wrote, describing the day of the attack. The "sky of cloudless blue, while the level, shimmering rays from the just-risen sun brought into fine relief, the splendid palms which here and there towered about the lower growth. The lofty and beautiful mountains hemmed in the Santiago plain, making it an amphitheatre for the battle."

The Spanish artillery began shelling the Americans at six thirty that morning. A piece of shrapnel hit Theodore's wrist, causing a welt. Six hours later, with the temperature above 100 degrees, the Rough Riders received orders from General Shafter's headquarters to advance on Kettle Hill.

"The instant I received my orders I sprang on my horse and then my 'crowded hour' began," the colonel recalled. As the Rough Riders marched along Camino

Real, the one road across San Juan Heights, they met the 10th Cavalry Buffalo Soldiers, an African American regiment, clustered on the road waiting for orders. Many of them joined the Rough Riders advancing on Kettle Hill as "Mauser bullets drove in sheets through the trees and the tall jungle grass."

Richard Harding Davis described the assault on Kettle Hill. Colonel Roosevelt, "the most conspicuous figure in the charge . . . mounted high on horseback, and charging the rifle pits at a gallop and quite alone, made you feel that you would like to cheer." Behind him hundreds of Rough Riders and Buffalo Soldiers "walked to greet death at every step, many of them, as they advanced, sinking suddenly . . . but the others waded on stubbornly, forming a thin blue line that kept creeping higher and higher up the hill. . . . It was a miracle of self-sacrifice, a triumph of bulldog courage . . ."

When he reached a row of barbed wire, Theodore jumped off his horse, scrambled over the wire, and ran up the last hundred feet. He and another soldier were the first Americans to reach the top. The Spanish troops had withdrawn to higher ground. As the rest of the Americans gathered on top of the hill catching their breath they came under heavy rifle from San Juan Hill. They fired back for several minutes before the colonel yelled for his men to join the troops some seven hundred yards away charging up San Juan Hill. The men swarmed up the hill and overran the enemy fortifications. Many of the Spanish soldiers chose to die in hand-to-hand combat rather than surrender.

After the battle, as the troops settled in for the night, one Rough Rider observed Colonel Roosevelt walking about San Juan Heights, "reveling in victory and gore." He appeared to be as happy as when he killed his first buffalo in the badlands. "Look at all of those damned Spanish dead," he said to one fellow New Yorker. TR later wrote that he enjoyed "the fragrant air of combat." The colonel thought he might have killed one man. He recalled emptying his revolver at two fleeing Spanish soldiers and seeing one "double up . . . like a jackrabbit." But he wasn't sure if one of his bullets or someone else's had killed the man.

There's no accurate count of American casualties for that day, the biggest battle of the Spanish-American War. The numbers range between six hundred to a thousand. Nearly one-fourth of the four hundred

Rough Riders were killed or wounded, a rate, Colonel Roosevelt bragged, higher than any other cavalry unit—it showed his men were in the middle of the action.

"For three days I have been at the extreme front of the firing line," TR wrote home. "How I escaped I know not." He did have several close calls. A rifle shot killed a messenger the colonel was talking to. And while he rode his mare, Texas, alongside a soldier, yelling at him to move faster, the man keeled over dead from a bullet. And early on the morning after the battle for San Juan Heights, an artillery shell hit near Colonel Roosevelt, killing several men but only showering him with dirt and gunpowder. "I really believe firmly now they can't kill him," marveled one Rough Rider.

On July 4 the six warships in Santiago's harbor attempted to break through the U.S. Navy's blockade, but they were quickly destroyed or captured. Then *insurrectos* and American soldiers lay siege to the city until the Spanish surrendered on July 17. Five months later, on December 10, Spain signed a treaty agreeing to give up the Philippine Islands, Cuba, and Puerto Rico, ending four centuries of Spanish colonialism in the New World. But way before then people in the

States were celebrating their newest war hero.

Accounts of Colonel Roosevelt leading his men up San Juan Heights appeared in numerous newspapers and magazines. Theodore was even nominated for the Medal of Honor, but never received it. No one knows exactly why. It might have been because he sent a letter to newspapers criticizing the secretary of war for not quickly bringing the troops home from the jungle, where some five thousand Americans died of typhoid, malaria, dysentery, and other diseases. Or it might have been because he called General Shafter "criminally incompetent." While not receiving the medal was disappointing, years later Theodore would declare, "San Juan was the great day of my life."

It was certainly a great day for his career. He wrote an account of the expedition that was serialized in a magazine and published in 1899 as a book titled *The Rough Riders*. Because Theodore wrote so much about himself in the book, one wag suggested the title should be *Alone in Cuba*. And being a war hero immediately boosted his political career. Even before leaving Cuba, the colonel was receiving telegrams urging him to run for senator or governor of New York. He returned home on August 15, and by September 27, he was the Republican candidate for governor.

As usual, Theodore ran an intense campaign. Escorted by several Rough Riders in uniform to remind the public the candidate was a war hero, he crisscrossed the state, making as many as twenty speeches a day. The Republicans were out of favor with New York voters because the current Republican governor had weakened state civil service laws and failed to clean up blatant corruption in state government. But on November 8, Theodore managed to win by a slim margin of 17,794 votes out of a total of 1,305,636.

As governor he soon angered political bosses and businessmen by supporting legislation requiring utility companies to pay state taxes. Theodore knew that coming out for the tax hurt his chances of running for a second term, because "no corporation would subscribe to a campaign fund if I was on the ticket." But he held firm to his position.

Observers began to talk of Governor Roosevelt as a presidential candidate. William Allen White, editor of *The Kansas City Star*, wrote that the governor was "more than a presidential possibility in 1904, he is a presidential probability. He is the coming American of the twentieth century."

But when Vice President Garret A. Hobart died on November 21, 1899, many Republicans supported Theodore for President McKinley's vice presidential candidate when he ran for reelection in 1900. Senator Tom Platt, the reigning political boss in New York, especially wanted Theodore to be vice president. He feared that two more years of him as governor would wreck the Republican Party in New York. All of the "high monied interests," TR explained to Senator Lodge, "that make campaign contributions of large size and feel that they should have favors in return are extremely anxious to get me out of the state."

But Theodore didn't want the new job. He told reporters he would "rather be in private life than be Vice President." The Constitution gives the vice president few responsibilities, other than replacing the president in case he dies or is incapacitated, and presiding over the U. S. Senate and functioning as a tiebreaker in case of a tie vote. In the end, though, despite his feelings, Theodore agreed to do what was best for the

Republican Party, and accepted the vice presidential spot. McKinley, running against Democrat William Jennings Bryan in his second presidential campaign, won by an 850,000-vote landslide in 1900.

After McKinley's inauguration on March 4, 1901, exactly one hundred years after George Washington had been sworn in as the first president of the new republic, the senate met for only four days before adjourning until the following autumn. Theodore wasn't sure what to do with all of his free time. "The vice president," he wrote, "is really a fifth wheel to the coach. It is not a stepping stone to anything but oblivion." That's no doubt what the Old Guard had hoped for Theodore, but things didn't turn out that way.

$\star$ $\star$ 8 $\star$ $\star$

ON SEPTEMBER 5, 1901, while President McKinley was attending the Pan-American Exhibition in Buffalo, New York, a man named Leon Frank Czolgosz stepped out of the crowd and shot him at nearly point-blank range. The bullets tore through his stomach and colon and lodged in the muscles in his back. Nine days later McKinley died, making Vice President Theodore Roosevelt the twenty-sixth president of the United States.

"It is a dreadful thing to come into the Presidency this way," TR wrote to Senator Lodge. "But it would be a far worse thing to be morbid about it. Here is the task, and I have got to do it to the best of my ability; and that is all there is about it."

Roosevelt with prominent naturalist John Muir in Yosemite Valley, California, 1903.

On President Roosevelt's first evening in the White House, Edith and the children were still at Sagamore Hill, so he invited Bamie and Corinne to come to Washington for dinner. It was September 23, Thee's birthday. He would have been seventy. "I feel that it is a good omen that I begin my duties in this house on this day," Theodore told his sisters. "I feel as if my father's hand were on my shoulder, and as if there were a special blessing over the life I am to lead here. What I would not give if only he could have lived to see me here in the White House."

Whatever awkwardness the president felt after McKinley's death quickly disappeared. "Now that I have gotten over the horror of the circumstances under which I came to the presidency," TR wrote to one of his uncles, "I get real enjoyment out of the work."

That was obvious to anyone who saw him. "His offices were crowded with people, mostly reformers, all day long, and the president did his work among them with little privacy and much rejoicing," the journalist Lincoln Steffens wrote. "He strode triumphant around among us, talking and shaking hands, dictating and signing letters, and laughing."

Theodore pledged "to continue absolutely unbroken the policies of President McKinley." He began by insisting that the men in McKinley's cabinet such as Secretary of War Elihu Root and Secretary of State John Hay keep their jobs. But, not surprisingly, the new president had his own ideas about what needed to be done.

High on Theodore's to-do list was to get himself elected president in his own right in 1904. His biggest obstacle was an Old Guard Republican named Mark Hanna, a U.S. senator from Ohio. Hanna, sixty-three years old, was a rich industrialist who had managed McKinley's ascent to the presidency. Soon after Theodore became president, Hanna reportedly exclaimed, "I told William McKinley that it was a mistake to nominate that wild man. . . . Now look, that damned cowboy is President of the United States!" And the senator later told Theodore straight out, "Theodore, do not think anything about a second term." Many people assumed Hanna, who was popular with businessmen and labor leaders alike, wanted the nomination himself.

Like other presidents before him, Theodore knew that he had to build a network of loyal Republican supporters to help him win his party's nomination in 1904. The president sent a dinner invitation to Booker T. Washington, an educator from Alabama and the nation's most influential African American leader. Theodore wanted advice on which southerners he should appoint to federal jobs. Apparently the president wasn't aware that no black person had ever been entertained in the White House. The October 16 dinner wasn't publicized, but a newspaperman scanning the White House guest book saw the familiar name and reported the event.

"President dines a darkey," shrieked a South Carolina newspaper. A Tennessee newspaper declared, "[t]he most damnable outrage ever perpetrated by any citizen of the United States." White southerners were angry because eating with a black person violated the segregated South's racial code.

"No one could possibly be as astonished as I am," Theodore said about the reaction. While privately calling his critics vicious idiots, he praised Washington as "a good citizen and good American," and insisted, "I shall have him to dine just as often as I please." But Washington received no more White House dinner invitations.

Theodore wanted to reassure Congress and Wall Street that he wasn't a reckless cowboy or hothead with his first major address to Congress. Unlike today, in Theodore's time, the president didn't give a State of the Union speech to a joint session of Congress. He sent his written address to the Capitol, where clerks read it aloud in each house.

The address, which is required by the Constitution, typically lays out the president's legislative aspirations; it's a kind of wish list. Unlike most presidents, Theodore wrote his own State of the Union after weeks of discussing the content with family, cabinet members, congressmen, and Wall Street friends. The president's eighty-page address touched on his major goals: more government oversight of business, federal protection of natural resources, a stronger navy, a canal across Central America, and a bigger role for the United States in international affairs. Nothing in the address set off any alarms. On the contrary, it seemed reassuring, as an editorial in the *New York Evening Post* explained: The "'Rough Rider' and 'the jingo,' the impetuous youth of a year ago, has disappeared." But time would tell.

While the president was busy reassuring the nation, newspaper reporters enjoyed writing about the tribe of Roosevelts in the White House. The staid mansion had never housed a president as young as Theodore, who had been only forty-two when McKinley was killed, or a family as large and rambunctious. They brought with them something TR called "the Oyster Bay atmosphere."

It was "the wildest scramble in the history of the White House. The children, hearty and full of spirits, immediately proceeded to cut loose," a servant named Ike Hoover recalled. There was "no tree too high to scramble to the top, no fountain too deep to take a dip, no furniture too good or too high to use for leap-frog and horseplay, no bed was too expensive or chair too elegantly upholstered to be used as a resting place for the various pets in the household." Along with six children ranging in age from four to seventeen came a menagerie of pets that included Jack the terrier, Sailor Boy the Chesapeake Bay retriever, Eli the macaw, a flying squirrel, Jonathan the piebald rat, two kangaroo rats, a parrot that screeched "Hurrah for Roosevelt," and a calico pony named Algonquin that the boys sometimes snuck up to their rooms on the second floor of the White House.

Ted was in his first year at the Groton School

and still trying to please his father. That autumn the skinny fourteen-year-old played a whole game of football despite a serious injury. "I was very sorry to learn that you had broken your collarbone," TR wrote, "but I am glad you played right through the game."

The president didn't want the newspapers to write about his children, but he had little control over Alice, who was nearly eighteen and loved the attention. Alice looked a lot like her mother—tall, blue eyed, and blonde. She was, declared *The New York Tribune*, "one of the prettiest girls in Washington." Newspaper reporters crowned her "Princess Alice," and she attracted more press coverage than any American except her father. The whole country read about how Alice carried a small green snake that she had named Emily, after her stepmother's sister. The nation knew the teenager smoked in public, bet on horses at the racetrack, and drove her friends' cars too fast. Her parents wouldn't let her have her own car. Nor would they let her smoke in the White House so when she wanted a cigarette she climbed out onto the roof. In mock exasperation Theodore once quipped to his novelist friend Owen Wister, "I can be president of the United States, or I can attend to Alice. I can't do both."

As for Edith, TR told a mutual friend, she "is too sweet and pretty and dignified as mistress of the White House and very happy with it." Some historians consider her the first "First Lady," in that Edith made the role of president's wife into a semi-official position. She sorted the mail each day and picked out letters needing Theodore's personal attention. He liked to respond to letters immediately and kept a team of stenographers busy. Edith managed Theodore's schedule, annoying uncles and cousins by insisting they make appointments. She also managed the White House's large staff of mostly African American servants.

Early in 1902, President Roosevelt fired the first shot across the bow of corporate America. The president told his attorney general, Philander Knox, to study a recent railroad merger that had created the Northern Securities Company. Theodore wanted to know if the new company violated the Sherman Antitrust Act, a little-used law Congress passed in 1890 making it illegal for companies to create trusts or monopolies that restrained trade or prevented competition.

John D. Rockefeller's Standard Oil Company had pioneered the trust thirty years earlier, and the new

The Roosevelt family, 1903.

business model had become common. In the case of
Northern Securities, J. Pierpont Morgan, James J. Hill,
and E. H. Harriman had owned the major railroads
between Chicago and the West Coast and had been
fierce competitors. But competition had proven so
unprofitable that the men agreed to combine their
companies into the Northern Securities Company—
and to coordinate rates in order to maximize profits.
It was the nation's biggest trust and was expected to
earn $100 million a year. Populists in the Midwest and

South hated trusts, especially those involving railroads, and called for the government to take them over. Well aware of the public's mood, Theodore had Knox file suit against Northern Securities, charging that the railroad company was an illegal monopoly.

Business consolidation and bigness were facts of life in the twentieth century, and Theodore had acknowledged that in his first State of the Union Address. But, "Great corporations exist only because they are created and safeguarded by our institutions and it is therefore our right and duty to see that they work in harmony with these institutions." It was "wicked . . . foolish," the president said, for businessmen to demand "immunity from governmental control."

It took over two years, but the Supreme Court decided Northern Securities was an illegal trust and had to be broken up. The court's decision didn't outlaw trusts, but it did subject them to more government regulation, which, at the time, was a novel—and to conservative businessmen and politicians a scary—idea. It was one of the big victories of Theodore's first term. While progressives applauded Theodore, the men on Wall Street talked about making Mark Hanna the next president.

Articles about the president's policies competed with articles about his antics. Newspaper reporters were fascinated by "the strangest creature the White House ever held." Theodore often went horseback riding through Rock Creek Park, a rugged natural area that runs through northwest Washington. He galloped along the trails taking potshots with his pistol at trees or stumps. Despite being guarded by the Secret Service, the president always, even in church, carried a pistol to defend himself. After all, three presidents—Abraham Lincoln, James A. Garfield, William McKinley—had been assassinated in his lifetime.

Theodore also liked to take his White House lunch guests, who were usually government officials and diplomats, on ten- to fifteen-mile hikes along the Potomac River and in Rock Creek Park. Sometimes they hiked in freezing temperatures or in the pouring rain. On one outing the president, the French ambassador, and several other men went skinny-dipping.

Theodore, everyone soon realized, was totally uninhibited. "You must always remember that the president is about six," observed Cecil Spring Rice, a friend and British diplomat. Because of his behavior, some people thought the president had a drinking problem.

"Theodore is never sober, only he is drunk with himself and not rum," wrote Henry Adams, a writer who lived on Lafayette Square across from the White House.

As the 1902 congressional races began heating up, so did labor problems in Pennsylvania, where, in May, over 140,000 coal miners walked off their jobs to start one of history's largest labor strikes. Coal mining was dirty, hard, and dangerous work. A typical miner could work ten to twelve hours a day, six days a week, and earned just $8 to $10 a week. The men, represented by the United Mine Workers (UMW), wanted shorter workdays and higher pay. Most significantly, the UMW—the largest union in the country—wanted the owners to do something they had never done before: to agree that the union had the right to represent the miners at the bargaining table. This last point seemed to be the most loathsome to owners.

"The coal presidents are going to settle this strike, and they will settle it in their own way," insisted George Baer, one of the most outspoken of the mine owners. "The rights and interests of the laboring man will be protected and cared for—not by the labor agitators," Baer declared, "but by the Christian men to whom

God in His infinite wisdom has given the control of the property interests of the country."

In past labor conflicts, the government had always sided with company owners. Just eight years earlier, at the request of railroad owners and over the objections of the Illinois governor, President Grover Cleveland sent thousands of federal troops to Chicago to force striking Pullman railroad workers back to work. But Theodore didn't think the federal government should take sides.

Yet as the price of coal rose from $5 to $20 a ton, the president began to worry about a "winter fuel famine." By late September many governors were urging Theodore to do something before cold weather caused misery and death for tens of thousands of people who wouldn't have coal to heat their homes. Some worried about riots. "Unless you end this strike," the governor of Massachusetts warned, "the workers in the North will begin tearing down buildings for fuel. They will not stand being frozen to death." Acting on a suggestion from the governor, Theodore asked the UMW president and the mine owners to meet with him in early October.

Just getting the six businessmen and the union

leader together in the same room was an accomplishment, since the owners insisted that neither the union nor any other "agitator" could represent their workers. The White House was undergoing major renovations, so the men met in a nearby town house. The president, dressed in a blue striped bathrobe, was in a wheelchair because weeks earlier while campaigning for Republican congressmen in Massachusetts, a trolley had smashed into his carriage, killing a Secret Service man and badly injuring Theodore's leg.

The president began the meeting with a brief statement. "The urgency and the terrible nature of the catastrophe impending requires me to use whatever influence I personally can. I appeal to your patriotism, to the spirit that sinks personal consideration and makes individual sacrifices for the general good."

John Mitchell, the UMW president and a former miner, immediately said he was willing to sit down with the owners to try to come to terms. If that failed, he would accept arbitration, or settling the disagreement with outside help.

But the owners responded by calling the miners "outlaws" and "instigators of violence and crime." The president became so annoyed with one particularly loud owner, John Markle, he later remarked: "If it wasn't for the high office I held I would have taken him by the seat of the breeches and nape of the neck and chucked him out of that window." The owners wouldn't budge, so the meeting ended quickly with no agreement in sight.

Theodore wanted the strike resolved before winter. "I could not see misery and death come to the great masses of the people in our large cities." He decided to declare a national emergency, take control of the coal fields, and send ten thousand soldiers to operate the mines. This plan was supposedly a secret, but, as Theodore no doubt intended, it was soon leaked to the newspapers.

When the mine owners read about the plan to seize their mines, they agreed to arbitration. The miners immediately went back to work, and soon there was plenty of coal. After several months of hearings and discussions, the five-man arbitration board decided the coal miners should receive a 10 percent pay raise. More significantly, it was the first time that a president had treated the concerns of workers equally with those of company owners. He later explained in a speech that it was important that the government not take sides in labor disputes because both sides deserved a "square deal." Theodore's first term as president became known as the Square Deal administration.

After the congressional elections in November 1902, when many Republican candidates won their races largely because Theodore had settled the coal strike, the president went bear hunting in Mississippi. In the first few days no one spotted a bear. His hosts, anxious for the president to have a successful hunt, finally captured a black bear, stunned it with a blow to the head, and tied it up. When Theodore saw the bear, which was about as tall as he was and only a few pounds heavier, he wouldn't shoot it; there was no sport in shooting a tied-up animal. He told the other men to put the bear out of its misery, and one of them killed it with a knife.

Later, *The Washington Post* published a cartoon of Theodore refusing to shoot the bear. It was a popular cartoon, and the cartoonist drew many others that included fat little bears with big ears. They gave a Russian Jewish immigrant named Morris Michtom of Brooklyn, New York, an idea. Michtom, who ran a toy shop,

Clifford Berryman's famous 1902 cartoon that linked Theodore and the teddy bear.

wrote the president asking for permission to use the name Teddy for a child's stuffed bear. "I don't think my name will mean much to the bear business," Theodore replied, "but you're welcome to use it." Michtom made a cuddly bear cub, called it "Teddy's bear," and sold it for $1.50. At about the same time F.A.O. Schwartz, the famous New York toy company, began importing stuffed toy bears from Germany, which then became known as Teddy bears.

Unlike many of his predecessors, the president took an active interest in international affairs. All "civilized and orderly powers," he said, should "insist on the proper policing of the world." The policing was especially important, Theodore felt, in North and South America.

The United States already had the three-quarters-of-a-century-old Monroe Doctrine, which forbade European nations from interfering in the internal affairs of or from colonizing newly independent countries in the Americas. The president expanded that doctrine in his 1904 State of the Union Address by adding what became known as the Roosevelt Corollary: "Any country whose people conduct themselves well can count upon our hearty friendliness. If a nation shows that it knows how to act with decency in industrial and political matters, if it keeps order and pays its obligations, then it need fear no interference from the United States." But, "chronic wrongdoing" or "general loosening of the ties of civilized society" will invite America's intervention. If this sounds a bit vague, it was. In practical terms, it was up to American leaders to decide if their neighbors were acting "civilized" or not.

The Pacific was another area that Theodore felt was important to the United States. He had long advocated annexing Hawaii before President McKinley did so in 1897. But about five thousand miles west of Hawaii, the Philippines was now proving to be a major problem for the president.

A year after acquiring from Spain in 1898 the seven thousand islands that comprise the Philippines, the United States began sending tens of thousands of soldiers—some 126,000 in all—to fight Filipino nationalists who resisted American occupation just as forcibly as they had resisted Spanish occupation. American officials explained that they wanted to impose "orderly freedom" and to "teach the people of the Philippines . . . how to make good use of their freedom." The United States occupied the Philippines for nearly a half century until finally granting independence in 1946.

Critics denounced the American occupation of the Philippines as needless expansionism and imperialism. Many Americans wanted their country to remain isolated from the world's problems. Others believed the country should acquire new territory and expand its power and influence around the world. As assistant secretary of the navy, Theodore had made it clear he was an unapologetic imperialist and expansionist. As president he had many more opportunities to exert America's influence abroad.

The Panama Canal, which the president considered "the great bit of work of my administration . . . one of the greatest bits of work that the twentieth century will see," was one of his more controversial accomplishments. On January 22, 1903, the United States signed a treaty with Colombia to lease—for $10 million up front and $250,000 "in perpetuity"—a six-mile swath of land across the Isthmus of Panama, which at the time was part of Colombia. After the agreement had been signed, Colombia's senate rejected it and demanded more money.

Mad at the Colombians for trying to "bar one of the future highways of the civilization," Theodore considered asking Congress to take the isthmus by force. While mulling over this option, he was visited on October 10 by Philippe Bunau-Varilla, a French engineer whose company had tried and failed to build a canal across the Panamanian isthmus. Bunau-Varilla told the president that, with a little help from the United States, a revolution making Panama a separate country could happen, and that the new country would readily agree to U.S. terms for a canal. Panamanians, isolated from Colombia by a mountain range, had tried many times to secede, only to be put down by the Colombian army, often with help from the U.S. Navy. Both TR and Bunau-Varilla insisted they made no specific deals in their meeting, but the president later observed that Bunau-Varilla "would have been a very dull fellow had he been unable to make such a guess." The president had tacitly agreed to support the revolution.

Madame Bunau-Varilla sewed together the first Panamanian flag in their New York hotel room, while her husband wrote the new country's constitution. The Frenchman had been told by the secretary of state that three U.S. warships would arrive in Colón, a city on Panama's Caribbean coast, on November 2 or 3. Bunau-Varilla, whose company would earn $40 million by selling the United States its construction equipment and other assets in Panama, sent $100,000 to cohorts on the isthmus and told them to declare independence from Colombia on November 3.

On the second of November, the USS *Nashville* dropped anchor in Colón and a squad of Marines marched into the city to prevent Colombian soldiers stationed there from stopping the Panamanians from declaring independence. The soldiers didn't put up a fight. Within forty-eight hours of the November 3 declaration, Theodore officially recognized the new government of Panama. The nation's first president declared, "The world is astounded by our heroism. Yesterday we were but the slaves of Colombia; today we are free. . . . President Roosevelt has made good."

In the spring of 1904, workers started digging the Panama Canal, which would connect the Caribbean Sea with the Pacific Ocean. When it was completed ten years later, the canal cut the distance ships had to travel from New York to San Francisco from fourteen thousand to six thousand miles. This greatly reduced the travel time between the east and west coasts for cargo, passenger, and navy ships.

As work on the canal got under way, Theodore was preparing for the Republican National Convention. Mark Hanna, the president's biggest obstacle to being nominated as his party's presidential candidate, had died in February. Theodore had no trouble winning the nomination that summer and little trouble winning election that November.

"Have swept the country by majorities which astound me," TR wired Senator Lodge. "I have the greatest popular majority and the greatest electoral majority ever given a candidate for president," he wrote Kermit. "My dear, I am no longer a political accident," Theodore told Edith.

Amid all of the celebration, President Roosevelt made what many observers believe was his biggest political blunder. "Under no circumstances," he announced, "will I be a candidate for or accept another nomination." The announcement shocked Theodore's supporters. George Washington had started the tradition of serving only two terms, and the president felt he was upholding that tradition. But most people thought that completing McKinley's term didn't count and that Theodore was eligible to run for another term in 1908.

His friends worried the announcement would hamper the president's effectiveness in the following four years, but Theodore wasn't.

$$\star \; \star \; 9 \; \star \; \star$$

"TOMORROW I SHALL come into office in my own right," Theodore crowed the day before his inauguration. "Then watch out for me!"

The president had his sights on problems both at home and abroad. For nearly a year he had been watching the war between Japan and Russia. It had started in early 1904 when Japan launched a surprise attack on Port Arthur, a new Russian seaport in southern China. Japan was a newly developing industrial nation that wanted to be dominant in the Far East, pretty much like Theodore wanted the United States to be dominant in the Americas. But Russia, already one of the world's major powers, had been aggressively expanding its presence and influence with Japan's neighbors, China and Korea. Japan went to war to stop Russia's expansionism.

Just after Theodore's inauguration in March 1905, the Japanese won a two-month-long battle in Manchuria, which is part of China, that cost the Russians 100,000 dead or captured soldiers. Then in May, Japan's navy ambushed the Russian navy at Tsushima Strait, between the Korean peninsula and the islands of Japan. The Japanese lost only three ships and 117 men, while destroying or capturing over two dozen Russian ships and killing or capturing an estimated 10,000 sailors.

"I was thoroughly well pleased with the Japanese victory," the president wrote to Kermit, who was at Groton. Theodore hoped Japan would check Russia's imperialist ambitions, but he also knew that Japan had ambitions of its own. "The Japs interest me and I like them," TR wrote to Cecil Spring Rice. "I am perfectly well aware that if they win out it may possibly mean a struggle between them and us in the future."

Theodore had been offering to mediate a peace agreement for a year when Japan, fresh from its naval victory, but short of money to continue paying for the war, accepted his offer. The president invited negotiators from both sides to meet in Portsmouth, New Hampshire, to work out an agreement. "I have led the horses to water," he remarked, "but Heaven only knows whether they will drink or start kicking one another beside the trough."

The negotiations soon bogged down. The Russians wouldn't agree to two of Japan's demands. The Japanese wanted an indemnity, or monetary settlement, and they wanted all of Sakhalin Island, which lies just north of Japan near the Russian mainland. They already occupied the southern half of the long, narrow island, which was rich in oil, coal, and other national resources. When the talks stalled, the president quietly went over the negotiators' heads to their leaders, Japan's Emperor Mutsuhito and Russia's Tsar Nicholas II. He got the two nations to agree to divide Sakahlin Island. Then the president urged the Russians to pay some indemnity, but they refused. He turned to the Japanese and persuaded them to drop their demand for money by pointing out that prolonging the war would be much more costly than losing the indemnity.

In early September, Japan and Russia formalized their peace agreement by signing the Treaty of Portsmouth. "It's a mighty good thing for Russia and a mighty good thing for Japan," President Roosevelt boasted, and "a mighty good thing for me too." The leaders of France, Great Britain, and Germany all congratulated the president and in Washington crowds cheered his success. The following year, 1906, Theodore was awarded the Nobel Peace Prize; he was the first American ever to receive that honor.

That summer, while the Roosevelts were visiting Sagamore Hill, there had been a security scare when a young man with a gun drove his carriage up to the gate and told the Secret Service guards he was there to marry Alice. There was a scuffle, and the man was taken away. The guards told the president that the intruder seemed mentally disturbed. "Of course he's insane," Theodore responded. "He wants to marry Alice."

Theodore didn't worry so much about the sanity of the man who did marry Alice in early 1907, but there were other concerns. His twenty-two-year- old daughter was marrying a rich Ohio congressman named Nick Longworth, who was fifteen years older than she. Edith and Theodore didn't approve of the age difference. They had recently dropped a friend who had married a woman twenty years younger; a "child wife" the Roosevelts called her. Another concern was

The president and his daughter, Alice, 1902.

Nick's reputation for drinking and chasing women, which must have made Theodore and Edith wonder if he would be another Elliott. But Alice's parents knew they couldn't keep their headstrong daughter from marrying Nick.

Before her wedding a reporter asked Alice what she needed in the way of wedding presents. "Trinkets. Preferably diamond trinkets," she replied. They weren't all diamond, but there were a lot of expensive gifts.

The Emperor of China sent earrings that were set with pearls and precious stones, the German Kaiser sent a diamond bracelet, and the Cuban government sent a string of pearls valued at $25,000. The bride received so many expensive gifts they needed a special room with an around-the-clock guard.

After her cousin Eleanor's wedding to Franklin Roosevelt a few months earlier Alice had quipped, "Father always wanted to be the bride at every wedding and the corpse at every funeral," because the wedding guests paid more attention to the talkative president than to the newlyweds. But at her ceremony Alice's father was not himself.

On February 17, hundreds of guests in the White House looked on as the Marine Band played the "Wedding March" and Theodore escorted his daughter down the aisle. The bride wore a white satin dress trimmed with old lace from her mother's wedding dress. She looked a lot like the first Alice, whose funeral had been twenty-two years and a day earlier. Instead of flashing his famous smile, Theodore looked grim and uncomfortable. No one knows for sure why he appeared upset. Perhaps it was because his daughter reminded him of her mother. Theodore never talked about his first wife after her death, even with his daughter, nor did he ever refer to her in any of his writings.

At the reception afterward Edith startled guests who heard her tell Alice, "I want you to know that I'm glad to see you leave. You have never been anything else but trouble." While most people thought she was joking, Alice wasn't so sure. But she didn't let it ruin the party as she borrowed a Marine's ceremonial sword to cut the wedding cake.

After the wedding the president prepared for a fight with Congress over several new regulatory laws. Many citizens wanted their government to provide more services and to regulate the economy to make life more orderly and stable. These people were part of a broad and diverse movement called Progressivism. It had started years earlier among the growing middle class in Chicago, New York, Boston, and other cities. Sick of what Theodore labeled the "unrestricted and ill-regulated individualism" of corporations, progressives were electing new congressmen and senators. Theodore, although more moderate than many, was the most visible and politically skilled progressive. Yet the older congressmen, with their years of experience and the support of big business, remained powerful and fought regulation of nearly every kind.

The president's legislative agenda got an unexpected boost that spring when the socialist author Upton Sinclair published *The Jungle*, a novel about the awful working conditions in the meat packing industry. But it wasn't the description of downtrodden workers that alarmed the public; it was the stomach-churning detail about how the sausages and canned meats sold to American families were made with diseased cattle, rats, and rat feces, or how the occasional worker who fell into a vat of boiling animal fat was processed and sold to housewives as "Durham's Pure Leaf Lard."

Government officials, at Theodore's behest, had recently conducted an investigation of the industry, and he knew conditions were even worse than Sinclair described. "The information given me seems to show conclusively that as now carried on the business is both a menace to health and an outrage to decency," he wrote to the chairman of the House Agricultural

Committee, urging "drastic and thoroughgoing" legislation. The public disgust spurred Congress to pass two bills the president supported. The Meat Inspection Act, which required federal inspection of packing plants, and the Pure Food and Drug Act, which established the Food and Drug Administration and gave the government authority to regulate foods sold across state lines.

The biggest fight between the president and conservative congressmen was over the Hepburn Act, a law giving the Interstate Commerce Commission authority to set "just and reasonable rates" for railroad shipping and to examine company financial records. The act would expand the ICC's regulatory power not only over railroads, but over other businesses as well. The "government ought not to conduct the business of the country," the president explained. "It ought to regulate it so that it shall be conducted in the interests of the public."

The railroads, the richest and most powerful companies in the nation, wanted to run their companies privately and their own way. They and their conservative allies in Congress fought regulation tooth and nail, while the president worked to organize bipartisan support. "The rate bill fight is dragging slowly along," he wrote Kermit. "I am now trying to see if I cannot get it through in the form I want by the aid of fifteen or twenty Republicans added to most of the Democrats." He complained that the Republicans wanted to take too much out of the bill, while Democrats wanted to put too much in. It was the president's persistent effort that got Congress to pass the Hepburn Act, which became law in the summer of 1906.

The president summed up his accomplishments in a letter to a friend. "It has been a great session. The railroad rate bill, meat inspection bill & pure food bill, taken together, mark a noteworthy advance in the policy of securing Federal supervision and control of corporations." One historian called the Hepburn Act "an historic event—the most important, perhaps, in Theodore Roosevelt's public career—and a not insignificant one in our national history."

The Wall Street businessmen who had contributed over $2 million in 1904 to help elect Theodore felt betrayed. Henry Clay Frick, a wealthy industrialist, complained, "We bought the son of a bitch and then he didn't stay bought."

Another noteworthy accomplishment during Theodore's second term was conservation. The president fought to protect as much of the country's natural resources as possible. "We are prone to speak of the resources of this country as inexhaustible; that is not so," the president pointed out in his State of the Union Address at the end of 1907. "As a people we have the right and duty," he said, "to protect ourselves and our children against the wasteful development of our national resources." Indeed, Theodore considered conservation "the fundamental problem which underlies almost every other problem of our national life."

More than any other president before him, Theodore relied on experts to help run the government. One of those experts was Gifford Pinchot, one of America's first professional foresters. He had graduated from Yale University and studied forest management in France before going to work for the U.S. Department of Interior in 1898. Seven years later Theodore appointed him the first chief of the newly created National Forest Service. Pinchot, one of few men to have floored the president during a boxing match, was Theodore's closest advisor on conservation.

The three previous presidents had placed 50

million acres into the National Forest Reserve, which was created in 1891 to protect forests from rapacious lumber companies. Theodore, acting on Pinchot's advice, placed 150 million acres into the national reserve before Congress, responding to protests from lumber companies and landowners, restricted the president's power to add to the reserve.

Few presidents before or since can match Theodore's record on the preservation and conservation of America's national resources. That record includes persuading Congress to create five new national parks such as Crater Lake in Oregon and Mesa Verde in Colorado. After Congress passed the Antiquities Act in 1906, which gives the president the power to protect areas of scientific or historical interests, primarily Native American ruins, by classifying them as national monuments, Theodore used that power to preserve unique natural areas that Congress was unwilling to protect. He saved Arizona's Petrified Forest from souvenir hunters and the Grand Canyon from mining companies by designating them national monuments. Later, Congress made both national parks. The president created a total of eighteen national monuments. Theodore, said Robert La Follette, a progressive

Wisconsin senator who later became a political rival, "did many notable things, but that his greatest work was inspiring and actually beginning a world movement for staying territorial waste."

While the president was saving national resources and regulating business, he also had his hands full regulating his sons. Quentin, who friends called "Q," was eight years old and attended public school, just as his older brothers had before going up to Groton. Theodore rarely whipped his children, even though at the time it was a common type of discipline. But he related to Kermit that Quentin had left "school without permission, and told untruths about it. I had to give him a severe whipping." Kermit was hardly a role model for his younger brother. At Groton, he was fighting with the headmaster, sneaking away from campus, drinking, and smoking opium. Ted, who was attending Harvard, was on academic probation. Plus, he had been roughed up and arrested after one of his friends struck a police officer. Senator Lodge had intervened to get Ted off.

The president's biggest challenge the following year was the economy. In March 1907, a major bank failed and the stock market declined 50 percent, plunging the country into a depression. Risky speculation and cutthroat competition among big banks was responsible, but Theodore's Wall Street critics said his new regulations had caused the trouble. The president responded in a speech by charging that "certain malefactors of great wealth" wanted "freedom from all restraint which will permit every unscrupulous wrongdoer to do what he wishes unchecked provided he had enough money."

When more banks failed that autumn and the economy looked as though it would get much worse, the president made a deal with his old foe, J. P. Morgan. A large coal and iron company in Tennessee teetered on the brink of bankruptcy. If it failed, it might cause banks and other businesses to fail, too. Morgan, who already owned many coal and iron properties, agreed to buy the company to save it from bankruptcy if the president promised not to prosecute him under the Sherman Antitrust Act. Theodore agreed. Morgan purchased the company at a bargain-basement price. Critics said Theodore, who had trouble balancing his own checkbook, had been duped.

Needless to say, Theodore didn't agree. "I am absolutely certain," he wrote Kermit, "that what I have done is right and ultimately will be of benefit to the country." He later insisted that "the result justified my judgment." The depression didn't get worse, but the criticism continued. Conservatives still blamed the economy's problems on his regulations, while progressives blamed him for making under-the-table deals with robber barons.

Some people were angry at the president, but he was a master at maintaining his popularity with the majority of Americans. Theodore distracted himself and the public from the troubled economy by sending the navy's new battleships around the world. Officially, the global cruise was a training mission, but it was also the largest display of naval power in history. The idea was to "speak softly and carry a big stick," an expression that had won him thunderous applause during a speech in Chicago in 1903. It meant that the nation should quietly pursue its interests, but be able to defend those interests if challenged.

"The Great White Fleet" consisted of sixteen battleships, dozens of smaller support craft, and eighteen thousand men. It got its nickname in the press because the ships had all been painted white, probably because it's the color of the internationally recognized flag of truce and indicated the navy's peaceful purpose. The fleet steamed out of Hampton Roads, Virginia, in December 1907 to begin a fourteen-month, forty-six-thousand-mile cruise around South America's Cape Horn, across the Pacific Ocean, though the Sea of Japan, into the Mediterranean Sea, and across the Atlantic Ocean back to Virginia. Theodore, watching from his presidential yacht the *Mayflower*, was as excited as a six-year-old. "Did you ever see such a fleet? Isn't it magnificent? Oughtn't we all feel proud?"

The president hoped the attention-getting voyage would not only advertise America's military strength but also encourage Congress to appropriate more money to build more warships. At first, Congress had refused even to approve money to pay for the Great White Fleet's mission. But the president told the legislators he had the money to send the fleet halfway around the world. If Congress wanted the fleet back, then it would have to appropriate more money.

After the ships disappeared over the horizon, the *Mayflower* cruised back up the Potomac River to Washington, where the president began to plan for the

1908 Republican National Convention in Chicago. Ironically, Theodore spent his first term making sure he would win his party's nomination and his second term making sure he wouldn't.

The president, as far back as 1905, felt that William Howard Taft should be his successor. After Root stepped down as secretary of war in 1904, Theodore had appointed Taft. "Taft is a splendid fellow," TR wrote Ted, "and will be an aid and comfort in every way."

People called the secretary "Big Bill" because he weighed over three hundred pounds, which was the subject of endless jokes. Upon hearing that Taft had been on a twenty-five-mile horseback ride, Elihu Root had asked, "How is the horse?" But Big Bill laughed off the jokes. Part of his appeal was his good nature. One person described him as "a huge pan of sweet milk."

Taft had studied law at Yale University and served as a federal judge. As "far back as I can remember," he said, "I believe my ambitions were of a judicial cast." More than anything he wanted to be chief justice of the Supreme Court. Even a few days before he was nominated to be the Republican presidential

TR was very physically active, even as president.

candidate, Taft said if he was offered the job of chief justice he would take it. But it wasn't only Theodore who wanted him in the White House. The secretary's wife, Helen, wanted to be First Lady more than her husband wanted to be president. But like many people, Helen was convinced the president would change his mind about a third term at the last minute.

Theodore himself related to an editor friend,

"There has never been a moment when I could not have had the Republican nomination with practical unanimity by simply raising one finger." He was too radical for some conservatives and too conservative for some progressives, but he was as beloved as ever by the American people. That was acknowledged even by his political enemies such as Democratic senator "Pitchfork" Ben Tillman of South Carolina, who said Theodore was "the most popular president the country has ever had."

At the Republican convention in June delegates paraded and chanted, "Four more years" and "We want Teddy," for more than three-quarters of an hour. But Senator Lodge, the convention's chairman, told the delegates, "His refusal of a renomination, dictated by the loftiest motives and by a noble loyalty to American traditions, is final and irrevocable." So Theodore's supporters gave up and supported Taft.

"Always excepting Washington and Lincoln," TR wrote to a British historian, "I believe that Taft as President will rank with any other man who has ever been in the White House." Of his own seven and a half years as president, Theodore said, "I have enjoyed every moment of this so-called arduous and exacting task." But he didn't change his mind about a third term, because "if there is any value whatever in my career, as far as my countrymen are concerned, it consists in their belief that I have been both an efficient public man, and at the same time, a disinterested public servant."

One of President Roosevelt's last official acts in 1909 was to join thousands of other people on George Washington's birthday, February 22, to watch the Great White Fleet return to Hampton Roads. The president attended despite having learned the day before that his nephew, Stewart, Corinne's youngest son and a Harvard sophomore, had died after plunging from his sixth-floor dormitory window. "I am heartbroken at the dreadful news," he explained to Archie. "No president can let any private matter interfere with a great public duty."

When the last of the ships cruised by the presidential yacht, the president told his military aid, "Another chapter is complete and I could not ask a finer concluding scene for my administrations." No other individual had done as much as Theodore to create this mighty navy. When he became president, the U.S. Navy was the world's fifth strongest. Now it was second to only Great Britain.

After Theodore left the White House, he remained one of the most popular people on the planet and, much to his old friend Taft's distress, increasingly critical of the new president.

★ ★ **10** ★ ★

THREE WEEKS AFTER Taft's inauguration in 1909, Theodore left the country for fourteen months to go on safari with Kermit in the east African country of Kenya. On his return trip, the former president passed through Europe, where he was greeted by large crowds and by heads of state. But no place gave him a bigger greeting than his hometown.

When the ocean liner carrying Theodore cruised into New York Harbor on June 16, 1910, it was met by hundreds of small craft, tugs, fireboats, and six navy battleships. They filled the air with the sounds of bells, whistles, and sirens and, from Fort Wadsworth on Staten Island, cannons boomed a twenty-one-gun salute. Tens of thousands of people, one of the biggest public gatherings in New York City's history at the time, filled the streets along the harbor, straining to see the familiar figure. When they saw Theodore on deck, said one observer, "such a shout went up from the shore as to waken the stones." Leading a parade up Broadway, the city's mayor and the former president rode in a black carriage followed by thirteen more black carriages of dignitaries, a band of Rough Riders on horseback, and a hundred-piece band.

For several weeks politicians visited Sagamore Hill to tell Theodore their concerns. Many complained that President Taft had aligned himself with the Old Guard Republicans. The colonel, as Theodore preferred to be called, had already heard some of the complaints. He had been deep in the jungle of Kenya when a barefoot messenger delivered a telegram informing him that President Taft had fired Gifford Pinchot from the National Forest Service. We "have just heard by special runner that you have been removed. I cannot believe it," TR wrote to his friend. "I do not know any man in public life who has rendered quite the service you have rendered."

Pinchot met Theodore in Italy that spring and gave him a list of complaints, which essentially said that the Taft administration wasn't following Theodore's policies, especially on conservation. The president had appointed a new secretary of the interior, Richard Achilles Ballinger, who seemed determinedly anticonservation. Pinchot had been fired for encouraging the press to write critical articles about Ballinger, who had been accused of working to give J. P. Morgan access to valuable government coal deposits.

These complaints were more serious than the irritating slights that had occurred after Taft's inauguration. First Helen Taft replaced several of the Roosevelts' favorite White House servants. Then, after implying that he planned to keep the members of Theodore's cabinet, President Taft replaced them all, mostly with conservative lawyers who had represented big business. Then the new president sent Theodore a thank-you letter saying he owed his successful election to both Theodore and Taft's older brother Charley, who had provided much of his campaign money. Theodore felt there was only one man responsible for Taft being president, and it wasn't Charley.

At times Theodore sounded like he was ready to live a quiet life as a contributing editor to *The Outlook*, a public-affairs magazine that paid him $1,000 a month. Although he was only fifty-one, he complained of feeling old. "Unfortunately my infernal body is bothered more or less with rheumatism," he said, "and I doubt if I shall be much good for long walks again." But the colonel wasn't about to retire from public life.

In August 1910, on a special train hired by *The Outlook*, Theodore began a sixteen-state speaking tour of the Midwest. While the former president insisted he was representing himself and no one else, his speeches probably had at least two purposes. He wanted to stir up enthusiasm for Republican candidates in the congressional elections that fall. And he wanted to promote his progressive ideas.

Theodore called these ideas the "New Nationalism," and he gave a speech in Osawatomie, Kansas, that spelled out exactly what the term meant. It "puts the national need before sectional or personal advantage," he explained. It means that the "citizens of the United States must effectively control the mighty commercial forces which they have themselves called into being." This required a strong federal government

Former President Roosevelt on his speaking tour, 1910.

to ensure social justice. He wanted laws that regulated the labor of women and children, limited the use of corporate funds for political purposes, and created income and inheritance taxes. The president should be the "steward of public welfare," Theodore said, while personal property was "subject to the general right of the community to regulate its use." The "essence of the struggle is to destroy privilege, and give to the life and citizenship of every individual the highest possible value both to himself and to the commonwealth." People in the Midwest cheered Theodore's ideas while people in the East denounced them as radical and communistic.

In the 1910 midterm elections the Republicans lost the House, which they had held since McKinley had been first elected president fourteen years before. And the party's Senate majority was reduced from twenty-nine to ten. Theodore blamed Taft for the midterm losses. "I am really sorry for Taft," he wrote one of his political friends. "I'm sure he means well, but he means well feebly, and he does not know how. He is utterly unfit for leadership, and this is a time when we need leadership."

The Colonel tried not to let politics interfere too much with his life at Sagamore Hill. "I have reveled in being home," TR wrote to a friend in Kenya, "and if fortune favors me I shall never again leave Mrs. Roosevelt and my own belongings." He was especially happy to learn that Ted and his wife, who had been married in June 1910 in Manhattan's Fifth Avenue Presbyterian Church, were already expecting their first child. "Home, wife, children, they are what really count in life," he wrote his son, who had moved to San Francisco after his wedding. "I have heartily enjoyed many things; the Presidency, my success as a soldier, a writer, a big game hunter and explorer; but all of them put together are not for one moment to be weighed in the balance when compared with the joy I have known with your mother and all of you. As merely a secondary thing, this house and the life here yield me constant pleasure. Really, the prospect of grandchildren was all that was lacking to make perfect mother's happiness and mine."

By the middle of 1911 Theodore's criticism of President Taft sharpened. He is "is a flubdub with a streak of the second-rate and the common in him, and he has not the slightest idea of what is necessary if this country is to make social and industrial progress."

Taft especially angered Theodore by advocating the use of arbitration to settle disputes between nations. In speeches, the president said the problems that had caused the Spanish-American War in 1898 and earlier foreign wars could have been settled peacefully if the two sides had sat down and talked. "I don't think," Taft explained, "that it indicates a man lacks personal courage if he does not want to fight, but prefers to submit questions of national honor to a board of arbitration."

Taft's ideas were "maudlin folly," Theodore snorted, because there were issues that could never be negotiated with Japan or Germany—the two nations he felt were the biggest threats to the United States.

"The truth is," Taft said of the ex-president's remarks, "he believes in war and wishes to be a Napoleon and die on the battlefield. It is curious how unfitted he is for courteous debate. I don't wonder he prefers the battle-ax."

Taft was also harder on the trusts than Theodore had been, and that caused problems as well. While the former president had been selective about which trusts to file suit against, Taft applied the letter of the law to all trusts. Theodore was especially irritated when Taft's attorney general filed suit against J. P. Morgan, charging that his acquisition of the Tennessee coal and iron company, which the ex-president had approved in 1907, had created an illegal trust.

By the beginning of 1912 Theodore had made up his mind. "Taft is utterly hopeless," he told a friend.

"I think he would be beaten if nominated, but in any event it would be a misfortune to have him in the presidential chair for another term, for he has shown himself an entirely unfit president."

Others agreed, and they knew exactly who they wanted to replace Taft. "Roosevelt for president" clubs sprang up across the country. The wealthy Wall Street businessman George W. Perkins offered to fund his campaign. Senator Robert La Follette, one of the country's prominent progressives, was already planning to challenge Taft for the Republican nomination, but several of his backers hinted that if Theodore ran they would switch allegiances. "I think well of La Follette," TR wrote Ted, explaining why he wouldn't support the senator for president. "With most of his policies I am in entire accord. He is, however, an extremist, and has the touch of fanaticism which makes a man at times heedless of means in attaining his ends."

After he decided to challenge Taft and La Follette for the Republican presidential nomination, Theodore explained that his previous misgivings about third terms applied only to consecutive terms. "Real danger would come from a man who had been in office eight years and may be thought to have solidified his power by patronage, contracts and the like, using that power to perpetuate itself."

Pinchot asked La Follette to step aside and let Theodore alone challenge Taft, but the senator refused. Many of his backers quickly jumped ship and climbed on board with Theodore. But the Colonel also needed support from moderate Republicans, and his policies were too radical for many of them.

One of Theodore's most controversial ideas had to do with judicial decisions. He was specifically concerned with popular laws passed by state legislatures, such as the attempts to regulate railroad rates back in the 1890s, which were struck down by the courts. If the courts issued an unpopular ruling, Theodore said citizens should be able to vote to reverse the ruling. Many moderates and conservatives denounced his idea as mob rule.

Theodore's candidacy against an incumbent Republican president upset Senator Lodge, his old friend of more than a quarter of a century. They had both agreed a long time ago that party loyalty was important. Now Lodge had to choose between being loyal to the Republican Party or to Theodore. "I have had my share of mishaps in politics," the senator wrote in a letter, "but I never thought that any situation could arise which would have made me so miserably unhappy." Lodge said he couldn't support Theodore, but he wouldn't oppose him either.

The Colonel's family rallied around him, though. He was amused when Alice, who always liked to thumb her nose at conventional behavior, came to visit. "I think she just had to see me because of course all respectable society is now apoplectic with rage over me," he told Kermit. Although Alice's husband Nick was running for reelection in Ohio and supported Taft, Alice backed her father's campaign "with mind heart and soul." Alice said her stepmother was "stony and unsympathetic" about Theodore's return to politics, but Edith eventually came around and said she was proud of her husband for "making an uphill fight for what he believes in." The "campaign is all that means anything to us now," said Theodore's youngest daughter, Ethel. She and several cousins worked as volunteers in her father's New York campaign headquarters.

The three-way race for the nomination inspired

lots of insults and name calling. In their editorials, newspapers said Theodore had the "daring of a madman" and "the instincts of a beast"; and he was "the most cunning and adroit demagogue that modern civilization has produced since Napoleon III." They believed his campaign was an "invitation to anarchy."

Taft said his former friend was "a dangerous egotist" and a "flatterer of the people. I hate a flatterer. I like a man to tell the truth." The president added, "Such extremists are not progressives—they are political emotionalists or neurotics."

"Mr. Taft only discovered that I was dangerous to the people after I discovered that he was useless to the people," Theodore responded. He labeled Taft a "fathead" and a "puzzlewit," which means stupid.

The ex-president was clearly the public's favorite. Party primaries were a new idea at the time, initiated by progressives so that ordinary people, rather than party insiders, could choose political candidates. States were slow to adopt the primary system, so there were only thirteen primaries in 1912. Theodore won them all—even the primary in Taft's home state of Ohio.

But Old Guard Republicans were still in control

of the party, and they awarded Taft a clear majority of the delegates to the June national convention in Chicago. Theodore's supporters disputed the eligibility of nearly half of those delegates. But the party leaders decided the matter by awarding most of the disputed delegates to Taft.

When Theodore heard about the decision, he rushed to Chicago to rally his supporters. In a speech he told them, we "fight in honorable fashion for the good of mankind; fearless of the future; unheeding of our individual fate; with unflinching hearts and un-dimmed eyes; we stand at Armageddon, and we battle for the Lord." He felt as fit as a "bull moose," he added. "We who are in this fight are not feeble, and we intend to carry the fight to the end."

The convention was wild. There were fist fights, noisy demonstrations, and cursing as the convention's chairman, Theodore's former secretary of war Elihu Root, asked each state for a voice vote. Knowing that he had lost the nomination before the vote was fin-ished, Theodore led his 344 delegates out of the con-vention shouting, "Thou shall not steal."

Over the next several weeks Theodore and his

followers decided to abandon the Republicans and formed the new Progressive Party. They returned to Chicago in August for their first convention. Circulars proclaimed: "At Three o'Clock Thursday Afternoon, Theodore Roosevelt Will Walk on the Waters of Lake Michigan." The ex-president didn't walk on water, but he did give another rousing speech. "The time is ripe, and overripe," he told the cheering crowd, "for a genuine Progressive movement, nation-wide and justice-loving, sprung from and responsible to the people themselves."

The presidential race was essentially between Theodore and the Democratic candidate, Woodrow Wilson. Taft did a little campaigning, but his heart wasn't in it. "There are so many people in the country who don't like me," he said at one point. Another time, after a speech attacking the ex-president, Taft told a reporter that "Roosevelt was my closest friend," and began to cry.

"My feeling is the Democrats will probably win if they nominate a progressive," Theodore had predicted privately. Their candidate was a progressive. Wilson had been a lawyer and professor of political science, president of Princeton University, and governor of New Jersey. The Democrat differed from Theodore in that he believed more strongly in state rights and was less concerned about labor laws and woman's suffrage. And he thought all trusts should be busted.

Theodore had hoped to win over progressive Democrats, but most were happy with Wilson. And when several important Republicans decided to remain loyal to their party and not join the Progressives, the Colonel felt his campaign was doomed.

Nonetheless, as he had done when he ran in the three-way race for mayor of New York in 1886, Theodore fought gamely. He portrayed both Taft and Wilson as puppets of political bosses and corporate tycoons. As always, the ex-president attracted big crowds— throngs of westerners stood for hours in the hot sun at train stops just to hear him speak for a few minutes as he traveled cross country. In Los Angeles, he drew a crowd of some two hundred thousand.

The campaign was cut short in Milwaukee on October 14 when a would-be assassin shot Theodore. With a bullet lodged in his chest, the candidate gave a remarkable hour-long speech to the crowd that was waiting at a nearby auditorium to hear him. Then aides rushed Theodore to the hospital. The chest wound was not life-threatening, but it was serious enough to keep him hospitalized for nearly a week and at Sagamore Hill for the last two weeks before the election.

On November 5, 1912, Woodrow Wilson won the election with 6.3 million votes; Theodore received 4.1 million; Taft received 3.5 million; and the socialist candidate Eugene V. Debs received 900,000 votes. "Well, we have gone down in smashing defeat," Theodore said. "I had expected defeat, but I had expected that we would make a better showing."

That winter at Sagamore Hill, as Theodore began to write a serialized autobiography for *The Outlook*, he felt "unspeakably lonesome." Was he finished with politics? "When it is evident," he noted, "that a leader's day is past the one service he can do is step aside and leave the ground clear for the development of a successor." But he had said he was through with politics back in 1883 after his first term in the New York Assembly. And he said it again in 1884 when he went west to raise cattle, and again in 1887 after he married Edith.

★ ★ 11 ★ ★

IN THE SUMMER of 1914, World War I, or the Great War as it was called then, began. While the conflict had roots in earlier quarrels between the great European nations, the spark that ignited the war was the assassination in June of Austria's Archduke Frances Ferdinand.

The main combatants were the Allied Powers of Great Britain, France, and Belgium and the Central Powers of Germany and Austria-Hungary. Before it ended, the war involved thirty-two nations and 65 million servicemen, of whom 20 million were wounded and 10 million killed. President Woodrow Wilson kept the United States officially neutral for three years, but German submarines kept sinking American cargo ships and killing American citizens, forcing the president to declare war on the Central Powers in April 1917.

One of Wilson's biggest critics was at Sagamore Hill writing magazine articles and a weekly newspaper column. Ever since he had written his book *The Naval War of 1812*, Theodore had stressed the importance of military preparedness, and he severely criticized Wilson for not adequately preparing the United States for World War I. He also criticized the president for not responding aggressively to Germany's invasion of Belgium in 1914, or to the German submarine attack a year later that sank the passenger ship *Lusitania* and killed 1,198 people, including 128 Americans. "I despise Wilson," Theodore told Bamie. And in another letter he said the Democratic president represented a "cult of cowardice."

The colonel, despite being fifty-nine years old, was eager to get into the fighting on the front lines in France. "I so strongly believe that where physical conditions will permit," he wrote to Kermit, "it is the old, the men whose life is behind them and who have drained the cup of joy and sorrow, of achievement and failure, who should be in the danger line, for the little sooner or the little later matters little to them."

Just as he had done in the Spanish-American War nearly twenty years earlier, Theodore wanted to recruit his own troops and lead them into battle. "I would literally, and gladly give my life to command a brigade of regulars under Pershing," he told a friend. "I could have raised four divisions (or eight divisions—200,000 men) of the finest fighting men and could have got them into the fighting line at the earliest moment." But Theodore didn't get the official approval he needed from President Wilson. Wars weren't fought that way anymore, he was told. For the first time the United States relied on a national draft to supply millions of soldiers.

While Theodore couldn't fight, his children could. "It's rather up to us to practice what Father preaches," Quentin told Owen Wister, the novelist and family friend. Ethel and her husband, a surgeon named Dick Derby, had already volunteered to go to Europe. In late 1914 they had left their toddler son with Theodore and Edith while they both went to Neuilly, France, to care for wounded Allied soldiers. And Ted's wife Eleanor volunteered to work with the YMCA providing rest and recreation services for Allied soldiers near the battlefield. With their encouragement, Theodore had pulled strings in Washington to get his sons good assignments. Ted and Archie got officers' commissions in General John Pershing's 1st Division, so they would be among the first American soldiers to see action. Kermit wanted to get into the fight even sooner. After his father appealed to British prime minister David Lloyd George, the British army gave Kermit a commission as a captain and sent him to Mesopotamia—which later became modern-day Iraq—to fight the Turks in a motorized machine-gun unit. Quentin, who was nineteen, had trouble with his eyes, so he memorized an eye examination chart to pass the physical exam and be accepted as a pilot in the Army Air Corps.

"It is a very hard thing on you four to go," Theodore explained to Archie. "It would be infinitely harder not to go, not to have risen level to the supreme crisis in the world's history, not to have won the right to stand with the mighty men of the mighty days." On Edith and Theodore's front porch a red-and-white service flag with five blue stars, one for each son or daughter serving the country, fluttered in the breeze.

❋   ❋   ❋

Theodore felt the nation needed a leader stronger than Wilson, and he wanted to be the Republican presidential nominee in 1916. He knew he couldn't win the presidency on a third-party ticket. Rejoining the Republicans was the only way. But the Old Guard wasn't ready to forgive the Colonel for deserting the party in 1912, so the Republicans nominated former New York governor Charles Evans Hughes to run against the Democrat incumbent. Hoping to mend fences and perhaps win the nomination in 1920, Theodore campaigned for Hughes. He didn't give twenty speeches a day as he had in 1912, but he still drew big crowds wherever he spoke. But he had mixed feelings about returning to the Republican Party. "The Republicans are a sordid crowd!" TR wrote to Corinne. "They are a trifle better than the corrupt and lunatic wild asses of the desert who seem most influential in Democratic counsels, under the lead of that astute, unprincipled and physically cowardly demagogue Wilson; but they are a sorry lot."

The Republicans narrowly lost the 1916 election. One reason the Democrats won was that many of the progressive reforms Theodore had advocated for during the campaign of 1912—such as a lower protective tariff, an income tax, regulations to stabilize the nation's banking system, and laws regulating corporations— were enacted during the first Wilson administration. In fact, the Wilson administration had been doing quite well until the war in Europe intruded.

After the president declared war, Theodore turned his attention to getting "the American people to think about its position and face its responsibilities." One observer called him "The Bugle That Woke America." He toured the country urging people to support the Red Cross and to buy Liberty Bonds, which were special bonds sold to the public to pay for the enormous cost of the war. Theodore himself bought some $60,000 worth of bonds.

In his zeal the Colonel often went overboard insisting on "one hundred percent Americanism" and complaining about "hyphenated Americans," as in German-Americans. "In this war either a man is a good American," Theodore declared, "and therefore against Germany, and in favor of the allies of America, or he is not an American at all." And he denounced

German and other foreign-language newspapers published in immigrant communities. "We must have one language," he insisted, "the language of the Declaration of Independence."

In many of his articles, Theodore attacked Wilson with such harsh language that friends warned him to button up. While he rarely cursed, one observer noticed he could say "pacifist" or "Woodrow Wilson" in tones that "would make the Recording Angel shudder." In the White House there was talk of bringing charges against Theodore under the 1918 Sedition Act, which made it a crime to "utter, print, write or publish any disloyal, profane, scurrilous, or abusive language about . . . the United States." But President Wilson said the best punishment was to ignore Theodore.

A mutual hatred of Wilson reunited Taft and Theodore. After the two ex-presidents had resumed corresponding, they ran into each other in a Chicago hotel and had a friendly half-hour talk. Theodore was no doubt impressed to hear that Taft's only son Charlie, who had been called Taffy as a child, had refused a commission, going instead to the front as an army private.

The Colonel often thought about his own sons. "I wake up in the middle of the night wondering if the boys are all right," Theodore said, "and thinking how I could tell their mother if anything happened." In a letter to Kermit he explained, "I am so very proud of the part that you boys have played. I should like to see all of you come home, and watch Mother's face as she greets you, and see you with your darling little wives and blessed babies."

In the summer of 1918, not long after receiving a letter from Archie saying that General William Sherman's famous pronouncement, "war is hell," was a "gross understatement," Theodore and Edith learned he had been severely wounded. Archie was awarded France's highest military honor, the Croix de Guerre, before being sent back to the States to heal. We have "a hero in the family," his father wrote to his wounded son. "You don't know how proud we are of you, how our hearts go out to you." Not long afterward, Ted was also wounded and awarded two military honors, the Distinguished Service Cross and Silver Star.

Theodore and Edith probably assumed they had a third hero in the making when they read in the newspaper that Quentin had shot down his first German plane. Theodore wrote Ethel that he was "immensely excited by the press reports of Quentin's feat." The next news about their youngest son came from a newspaper reporter who told them Quentin had gotten separated from his squad, attacked by seven German Fokkers, and went down behind enemy lines. No one knew if he had been captured or killed. Several days later the Germans reported he was dead.

Theodore attempted to appear brave. No "man could have died in finer or more gallant fashion," he told Kermit, "and our pride equals our sorrow." He tried to keep busy dictating letters despite, his secretary later related, "his voice choking with emotion . . . and the tears streaming down his face." Theodore would mumble "Poor Quinikins" to himself when he thought no one could hear.

Quentin's death saddened him as much as Alice's had thirty-four years earlier. But back then Theodore had been young and resilient. Now he wasn't. "I feel as though I were a hundred years old," he complained, "and had *never* been young."

Nonetheless, the Colonel still wanted to be president again. After voters rebuffed President Wilson and the Democrats in the November 1918 midterm elections by sending Republican majorities to both houses of Congress, party leaders wanted to know if Theodore would accept the presidential nomination in 1920. If "I am the man the people want," he responded, "I don't see how I could refuse to run." But it was not to be.

The American soldiers pouring into France had tipped the balance of power in favor of the Allies. On "the eleventh hour of the eleventh day of the eleventh month of 1918" the Allies and Germany signed an armistice, ending the fighting in Europe. That same day, Theodore went into the hospital. "Father is flat on his back with gout," Edith reported to Ted. "He is having a horrid suffering time." He stayed in the hospital seven weeks, returning home just before Christmas.

On January 5, 1919, Theodore worked eleven hours finishing up a newspaper column and proofreading one of his magazine articles. Late in the day while watching the "dancing of the waves" on Long Island Sound, Edith said he "spoke of the happiness of being home" and asked, "I wonder if you will ever know how I love Sagamore Hill."

That evening, after reading a bit and making notes to himself about things to do the next day, Theodore said to his valet, "James, will you please put out the light." He died early the next morning of a coronary embolism. Archie's cable to Ted and Kermit in Europe simply stated, "The old lion is dead."

A tribute Theodore had written for Quentin applies to the "old lion" just as well: "Only those are fit to live who do not fear to die. And none are fit to die who have shrunk from the joy of life and the duty of life. Both life and death are parts of the same Great Adventure."

The story of Theodore Roosevelt didn't end with his death. His legacy survives in our national parks and forests. It survives in a strong federal government that serves and protects all Americans. It survives in the power of every U.S. president to shape events at home and around the world. And it survives atop Mount Rushmore in South Dakota, where the granite sculptures of four of our greatest presidents—George Washington, Thomas Jefferson, Abraham Lincoln, and Theodore Roosevelt—gaze out over the nation they served so well.

Mount Rushmore near completion, 1941.

SOURCE NOTES

INTRODUCTION

"As I did . . .": Brands, *T.R.*, 721.

"Stand back . . ." and "Don't hurt that. . .": Miller, *A Life*, 530.

"Friends I shall . . ." and "There is a . . .": Brands, *T.R.*, 721.

CHAPTER 1

"I owe everything . . .": Dalton, *Strenuous*, 50.

"He was interested . . .": Roosevelt, *Autobiography*, 9.

"nobody seemed to . . .": Dalton, *Strenuous*, 35.

"I could breathe . . .": Morris, *The Rise*, 11.

"have the mind . . .": Brands, *T.R.*, 26.

"got my first . . .": Morris, *The Rise*, 34.

"he had done . . ." and "every other feeling . . .": Dalton, *Strenuous*, 27.

"If you offered . . .": Miller, *A Life*, 42.

"Worshipped *Little Men* . . ." and "girls' stories": Roosevelt, *Autobiography*, 14.

"great admiration for . . .": Brands, *T.R.*, 28.

"the very best . . ." and "manliness, decency, and . . .": Brands, *T.R.*, 27.

"he swore like . . .": Harbaugh, *Power*, 10.

"cordially hated": Brands, *T.R.*, 25.

"The young man . . .": Brands, *T.R.*, 49.

"Roosevelt of New York": Miller, *A Life*, 66.

"Out-of-doors natural history": Roosevelt, *Autobiography*, 25.

"That seal filled . . .": Miller, *A Life*, 39.

"utterly ignored the . . .": Roosevelt, *Autobiography*, 26.

"I felt as . . .": Brands, *T.R.*, 81.

"The one I . . .": Brands, *T.R.*, 82.

"I almost feel . . ." and "as distinctly as. . .": McCullough, *Mornings*, 187.

"With the help . . .": Brands, *T.R.*, 81.

"I wonder who . . .": McCullough, *Mornings*, 191.

"I care for . . .": Dalton, *Strenuous*, 79.

"My happiness is . . .": Morris, *The Rise*, 113.

"a kind of club-room": Roosevelt, *Autobiography*, 58.

"deplorable lack of . . .": Brands, *T.R.*, 144.

"rough and brutal . . .": Roosevelt, *Autobiography*, 57.

"be of the . . .": Roosevelt, *Autobiography*, 57.

CHAPTER 2

"Suddenly our eyes . . ." and "His hair was. . .": Morris, *The Rise*, 144.

"Society man and . . ." and "kid glove, scented . . .": Dalton, *Strenuous Life*, 81.

"huge, fleshy, unutterably . . .": Brands, *T.R.*, 150.

"By God if . . .": Morris, *The Rise*, 149.

"Won't Mama's boy . . ." and "knocked him down . . .": Morris, *The Rise*, 149.

"either dumb or . . .": McCullough, *Mornings*, 255.

"a stupid, sodden . . .": Morris, *The Rise*, 145.

"an average balloon" and "entirely unprincipled, with . . .": Brands, *T.R.*, 131.

"an ungreased squeak": McCullough, *Mornings*, 160.

"mister spee-kar . . .": Morris, *The Rise*, 153.

"wasn't anything cool . . .": Miller, *A Life*, 136.

"a trait of . . .": McCullough, *Mornings*, 276.

"would come into . . .": Brands, *T.R.*, 141.

"the Cyclone Assemblyman": Morris, *The Rise*, 163.

"willing to go . . .": Miller, *A Life*, 132.

"sharks" and "swindlers" and "men whose financial . . .": Miller, *A Life*, 133.

"of vital importance . . ." "like the bursting . . ." and "a dead silence . . .": Pringle, *Theodore*, 50.

"I have drawn . . .": Miller, *A Life*, 135.

"a boldness that . . .": Brands, *T.R.*, 137.

"Mr. Roosevelt accomplished . . .": Pringle, *Theodore*, 52.

"has a most . . ." and "a splendid career": Miller, *A Life*, 134.

"evil and heart . . .": Brands, *T.R.*, 133.

"leave politics" "with the right . . ." "control others and . . ." and "the first glimpse . . .": Morris, *The Rise*, 158.

"ideal . . . We hailed . . .": Morris, *The Rise*, 162.

CHAPTER 3

"I have become . . .": Morris, *The Rise*, 138.

"the teachings of . . .": Brands, *T.R.*, 125.

"I felt as . . .": Miller, *A Life*, 145.

"wealthy criminal class": Morris, *The Rise*, 177.

"the arch thief . . .": Harbaugh, *Power*, 20.

"rose like a rocket": Miller, *A Life*, 140.

"a political ascent . . .": Morris, *The Rise*, 169.

"a very desolate . . .": Brands, *T.R.*, 153.

"I am now . . .": Brands, *T.R.*, 155.

"Of course I . . ." "Hurrah! The luck . . ." and "This has been . . .":
    Brands, *T.R.*, 158.

"the romance of . . .": Morris, *The Rise*, 200.

"There is a curse . . .": Morris, *The Rise*, 229.

"Theodore is in . . .": Morris, *The Rise*, 231.

"For joy or . . .": Dalton, *Strenuous*, 89.

"I shall go . . .": Dalton, *Strenuous*, 90.

"Tammany Defeated: Mr. . . .": Morris, *The Rise*, 221.

"I have very . . .": Morris, *The Rise*, 248.

"I am going . . .": Morris, *The Rise*, 259.

CHAPTER 4

"far off from . . .": Morris, *The Rise*, 259.

"Having a glorious . . .": Brands, *T.R.*, 172.

"I wear a . . .": Brands, *T.R.*, 173.

"defective moral character": Harbaugh, *Power*, 48.

"When I went . . .": Morris, *The Rise*, 295.

"Hasten forward quickly there": Harbaugh, *Power*, 49.

"a purty rider": Harbaugh, *Power*, 48.

"I have been three . . .": Brands, *T.R.*, 189.

"Four eyes is . . ." and "Well if I've . . .": Harbaugh, *Power*, 48.

"Cocking my rifle . . .": Brands, *T.R.*, 175.

"There were all . . .": McCullough, *Mornings*, 336.

"the still, merciless . . .": Morris, *The Rise*, 288.

"I shall call . . .": Dalton, *Strenuous*, 89.

"that keenest of . . .": Morris, *The Rise*, 291.

"sweet manner": Morris, *The Rise*, 309.

"air of softness . . ." and "You have no . . .": Morris, *The Rise*, 358.

"Edith we have . . .": Dalton, *Strenuous*, 107.

"I utterly disbelieve . . .": Dalton, *Strenuous*, 106.

"You could not . . .": Brands, *T.R.*, 201.

"He is one . . .": Harbaugh, *Power*, 62.

"major part of . . .": Dalton, *Strenuous*, 95.

"one of the . . .": Harbaugh, *Power*, 48.

CHAPTER 5

"we love a . . .": Dalton, *Strenuous*, 133.

"If you wish . . .": Brands, *T.R.*, 202.

"The boy is . . .": Brands, *T.R.*, 216.

"too sweet and . . .": Brands, *T.R.*, 217.

"one of the . . .": Miller, *A Life*, 131.

"drank like a . . .": Miller, *A Life*, 130.

"literary feller": Miller, *A Life*, 201.

"I shall probably . . .": Morris, *The Rise*, 391.

"tinglingly alive, masculine . . .": Harbaugh, *Power*, 51.

"writing is horribly . . .": Brands, *T.R.*, 212.

"write some book . . .": Brands, *T.R.*, 214.

"swinish butchers": Morris, *The Rise*, 387.

"I do fear . . .": Harbaugh, *Power*, 74.

CHAPTER 6

"first a good . . .": Morris, *The Rise*, 407.

159,356 federal jobs: Historical Statistics of the United States.

"I am a . . .": Harbaugh, *Power*, 75.

"Alice needs someone . . .": Brands, *T.R.*, 235.

"nightmare of horror": Morris, *The Rise*, 438.

"It is horrible . . .": Morris, *The Rise*, 440.

"is to do the work . . .": Morris, *The Rise*, 446.

"Elliott Roosevelt Insane . . .": Morris, *The Rise*, 452.

"What a hideous . . .": Brands, *T.R.*, 247.

"settle the thing . . .": Brands, *T.R.*, 249.

"hypocritical haberdasher!": Morris, *The Rise*, 413.

"The exposure he . . .": Morris, *The Rise*, 464.

"His colleagues were . . .": Harbaugh, *Power*, 77.

"are handed down . . .": Harbaugh, *Power*, 76.

"Elliott has sunk . . ." "I do wish . . ." and "more overcome than . . .": Brands, *T.R.*, 259.

"I used to . . .": Miller, *A Life*, 215.

"I must make . . .": Harbaugh, *Power*, 82.

"We have a . . ." and "he has great . . .": Harbaugh, *Power*, 83.

"closing all of . . .": Harbaugh, *Power*, 84.

"A taste for . . .": Brands, *T.R.*, 299.

"You may easily . . .": Brands, *T.R.*, 302.

CHAPTER 7

"To prepare for . . .": Miller, *A Life*, 254.

"We need a . . .": Miller, *A Life*, 253.

"I hope to . . .": Morris, *The Rise*, 624.

"We ought to . . .": Morris, *The Rise*, 545.

"The secretary is . . .": Miller, *A Life*, 257.

"The decks are . . .": Miller, *A Life*, 258.

"I did not . . .": Harbaugh, *Power*, 95.

"the instigator of . . .": Dalton, *Strenuous*, 135.

"I want my . . .": Dalton, *Strenuous*, 558.

"to be all . . .": Dalton, *Strenuous*, 171.

"never press Ted . . .": Brands, *T.R.*, 336.

"an act of . . .": Morris, *The Rise*, 627.

"Blood on the . . .": Miller, *A Life*, 259.

"To Hell with . . .": Miller, *A Life*, 271.

"the policy of . . .": Morris, *The Rise*, 630.

"offensive operations in . . .": Morris, *The Rise*, 629.

"During my short . . .": Morris, *The Rise*, 630.

"If I am . . .": Miller, *A Life*, 173.

"I have a . . .": Brands, *T.R.*, 333.

"has lost his . . .": Morris, *The Rise*, 644.

"I know now . . .": Miller, *A Life*, 273.

"He felt he . . .": Dalton, *Strenuous*, 171.

"as typical an . . .": Brands, *T.R.*, 341.

"The folly, the . . .": Morris, *The Rise*, 639.

"Yesterday we struck . . .": Brands, *T.R.*, 349.

"fight really was . . .": Morris, *The Rise*, 676.

"It was a . . .": Brands, *T.R.*, 352.

"The instant I . . ." and "Mauser bullets drove . . .": Brands, *T.R.*, 353.

"the most conspicuous . . .": Brands, *T.R.*, 356.

"walked to greet . . .": Miller, *A Life*, 303.

"reveling in victory . . ." and "Look at all . . .": Morris, *The Rise*, 687.

"the fragrant air . . .": Morris, *The Rise*, 688.

"double up . . . like . . .": Miller, *A Life*, 304.

"For three days . . .": Miller, *A Life*, 305.

"I really believe . . .": Morris, *The Rise*, 688.

"criminally incompetent": Morris, *The Rise*, 659.

"San Juan was . . .": Brands, *T.R.*, 357.

"no corporation would . . .": Harbaugh, *Power*, 166.

"more than a . . .": Miller, *A Life*, 331.

"high monied interests . . .": Miller, *A Life*, 337.

"rather be in . . .": Miller, *A Life*, 338.

"The vice president . . .": Miller, *A Life*, 346.

CHAPTER 8

"It is a . . .": Brands, *T.R.*, 418.

"I feel that . . .": Dalton, *Strenuous*, 207.

"I feel as . . .": Morris, *Rex*, 46.

"Now that I . . .": Dalton, *Strenuous*, 221.

"His offices were . . .": Miller, *A Life*, 359.

"to continue absolutely . . .": Brands, *T.R.*, 418.

"I told William . . .": Brinkley, *American History*, 642.

"Theodore do not . . .": Morris, *Rex*, 39.

"President dines a . . .": Morris, *Rex*, 55.

"the most damnable . . ." "No one could . . ." and "a good citizen . . .":
  Brands, *T.R.*, 423.

"The "'Rough Rider' . . .": Brands, *T.R.*, 430.

"the Oyster Bay . . .": Morris, *Rex*, 43.

"the wildest scramble . . ." and "no tree too . . .": Eyewitnesstohistory.
  com.

"Hurrah for Roosevelt": Miller, *A Life*, 414.

"I was very . . .": Brands, *T.R.*, 431.

"one of the . . .": Cordery, *Alice*, 51.

"I can be . . .": Brands, *T.R.*, 521.

"is too sweet . . .": Brands, *T.R.*, 433.

"Great corporations exist . . .": Morris, *Rex*, 73.

"wicked . . . foolish": Brands, *T.R.*, 438.

"the strangest creature . . .": Morris, *Rex*, 108.

"You must always . . .": Morris, *Rex*, 81.

"Theodore is never . . .": Morris, *Rex*, 82.

"The coal presidents . . .": Morris, *Rex*, 133.

"The rights and . . .": Brands, *T.R.*, 457.

"winter fuel famine": Morris, *Rex*, 152.

"Unless you end . . .": Morris, *Rex*, 51.

"The urgency and . . .": Brands, *T.R.*, 454.

"outlaws" and "instigators of violence . . .": Brands, *T.R.*, 457.

"If it wasn't . . .": Brands, *T.R.*, 455.

"I could not . . .": Miller, *A Life*, 374.

"I don't think . . .": Miller, *A Life*, 423.

"civilized and orderly . . .": Miller, *A Life*, 385.

"Any country whose . . .": Brands, *T.R.*, 526.

"chronic wrongdoing" and "general loosening of . . .": Brands, *T.R.*, 543.

"orderly freedom" and "teach the people . . .": Morris, *Rex*, 110.

"the great bit . . .": Morris, *Rex*, 116.

"bar one of . . .": Brands, *T.R.*, 482.

"would have been . . ." and "The world is . . .": Miller, *A Life*, 406.

"Have swept the . . .": Brands, *T.R.*, 513.

"I have the . . .": Miller, *A Life*, 435.

"My dear, I . . .": Miller, *A Life*, 436.

"Under no circumstances . . .": Brands, *T.R.*, 514.

CHAPTER 9

"Tomorrow I shall . . .": Dalton, *Strenuous*, 271.

"I was thoroughly . . ." and "The Japs interest . . .": Brands, *T.R.*, 531.

"I have led . . .": Dalton, *Strenuous*, 284.

"It's a mighty . . .": Morris, *Rex*, 414.

"Of course he's . . .": Brands, *T.R.*, 558.

"child wife": Dalton, *Strenuous*, 278.

"Trinkets. Preferably diamond . . .": Morris, *Rex*, 436.

"Father always wanted . . .": Encarta, 802.

"I want you . . .": Morris, *Rex*, 437.

"unrestricted and ill-regulated . . .": Harbaugh, *Power*, 522.

"'Durham's Pure Leaf Lard'": Miller, *A Life*, 460.

"The information given . . ." and "drastic and thoroughgoing": Brands, *T.R.*, 550.

"government ought not . . .": Miller, *A Life*, 464.

"The rate bill . . .": Brands, *T.R.*, 547.

"It has been . . .": Miller, *A Life*, 462.

"an historic event": Harbaugh, *Power*, 252.

"We bought the . . .": Miller, *A Life*, 440.

"We are prone . . .": Brands, *T.R.*, 624.

"the fundamental problem . . .": Dalton, *Strenuous*, 338.

"did many notable . . .": Morris, *Rex*, 338.

"school without permission . . .": Kraft, *Champion*, 127.

"certain malefactors of . . .": Brands, *T.R.*, 619.

"I am absolutely . . .": Morris, *Rex*, 501.

"The result justified . . .": Miller, *A Life*, 478.

"speak softly and . . .": Morris, *Rex*, 215.

"Did you ever . . .": Brands, *T.R.*, 613.

"Taft is a . . .": Brands, *T.R.*, 594.

"How is the . . .": Brands, *T.R.*, 593.

"a huge pan . . .": Morris, *Rex*, 543.

"far back as . . .": Morris, *Rex*, 308.

"There has never . . .": Brands, *T.R.*, 626.

"the most popular . . .": Morris, *Rex*, 430.

"Four more years" and "We want Teddy": Morris, *Rex*, 525.

"His refusal of . . .": Brands, *T.R.*, 627.

"Always excepting Washington . . .": Brands, *T.R.*, 628.

"I have enjoyed . . .": Dalton, *Strenuous*, 344.

"if there is . . .": Morris, *Rex*, 527.

"I am heartbroken . . .": Brands, *T.R.*, 636.

"Another chapter is . . .": Morris, *Rex*, 549.

CHAPTER 10

"such a shout . . .": Brands, *T.R.*, 669.

"have just heard . . .": Harbaugh, *Power*, 387.

"Unfortunately my infernal . . .": Brands, *T.R.*, 687.

"puts the national . . .": Harbaugh, *Power*, 368.

"citizens of the . . .": Brands, *T.R.*, 676.

"steward of public welfare": Brinkley, *American History*, 649.

"essence of the . . .": Harbaugh, *Power*, 367.

"I am really . . .": Brands, *T.R.*, 698.

"I have reveled . . .": Brands, *T.R.*, 686.

"Home, wife, children . . .": Brands, *T.R.*, 682.

"is a flubdub . . .": Harbaugh, *Power*, 399.

"I don't think . . .": Harbaugh, *Power*, 401.

"maudlin folly" and "The truth is . . .": Harbaugh, *Power*, 400.

"Taft is utterly . . .": Miller, *A Life*, 521.

"I think well . . ." and "With most of . . .": Brands, *T.R.*, 683.

"Real danger would . . .": Harbaugh, *Power*, 413.

"I have had . . .": Brands, *T.R.*, 706.

"I think she . . .": Brands, *T.R.*, 710.

"with mind heart . . .": Dalton, *Strenuous*, 381.

"stony and unsympathetic" and "making an uphill . . .": Dalton,
    Strenuous, 387.

"campaign is all . . .": Dalton, *Strenuous*, 386.

"daring of a . . ." "the instincts of . . ." "the most cunning . . ." and
    "invitation to anarchy": Dalton, *Strenuous*, 385.

"a dangerous egotist" and "flatterer of the . . .": Brands, *T.R.*, 712.

"Such extremists are . . .": Brands, *T.R.*, 709.

"Mr Taft only . . .": Dalton, *Strenuous*, 388.

"fathead" and "puzzlewit": Brands, *T.R.*, 712.

"fight in honorable . . .": Dalton, *Strenuous*, 389.

"bull moose": Miller, *A Life*, 525.

"We who are . . .": Brands, *T.R.*, 714.

"Thou shall not steal": Harbaugh, *Power*, 435.

"At Three o'Clock . . ." and "The time is . . .": Brands, *T.R.*, 719.

"There are so . . .": Brinkley, *American History*, 653.

"Roosevelt was my . . .": Brands, *T.R.*, 707.

"My feeling is . . .": Brands, *T.R.*, 717.

"Well, we have . . .": Brands, *T.R.*, 725.

"unspeakably lonesome": Dalton, *Strenuous*, 408.

"When it is . . .": Miller, *A Life*, 532.

CHAPTER 11

"I despise Wilson": Brands, *T.R.*, 773.

"cult of cowardice": Dalton, *Strenuous*, 458.

"I so strongly . . .": Brands, *T.R.*, 786.

"I would literally . . .": Brands, *T.R.*, 784.

"It's rather up . . .": Miller, *A Life*, 557.

"It is a . . .": Brands, *T.R.*, 786.

"The Republicans are . . .": Brands, *T.R.*, 773.

"the American people . . .": Brands, *T.R.*, 766.

"The Bugle That . . .": Miller, *A Life*, 542.

"one hundred percent Americanism": Miller, *A Life*, 558.

"hyphenated Americans": Brands, *T.R.*, 762.

"In this war . . ." and "We must have . . .": Miller, *A Life*, 558.

"pacifist" "Woodrow Wilson" and "would make the . . .": Miller, *A Life*, 544.

"utter, print, write . . .": www.u-s-history.com.

"I wake up . . .": Miller, *A Life*, 560.

"I am so . . .": Brands, *T.R.*, 796.

"war is hell" and "gross understatement": Dalton, *Strenuous*, 495.

"a hero in . . ." and "You don't know . . .": Brands, *T.R.*, 792.

"immensely excited by . . .": Miller, *A Life*, 561.

"man could have . . .": Brands, *T.R.*, 800.

"his voice choking . . .": Brands, *T.R.*, 799.

"Poor Quinikins": Brands, *T.R.*, 802.

"I feel as . . .": Miller, *A Life*, 560.

"I am the . . .": Miller, *A Life*, 564.

"the eleventh hour . . .": Neiberg, *Fighting*, 361.

"Father is flat . . .": Miller, *A Life*, 564.

"dancing of the . . ." and "spoke of the . . .": Miller, *A Life*, 565.

"James, will you . . .": Brands, *T.R.*, 811.

"old lion": Miller, *A Life*, 566.

"Only those are . . .": Brands, *T.R.*, 815.

BIBLIOGRAPHY

Blum, John Morton. *The Republican Roosevelt*. Cambridge: Harvard University Press, 1954.

Brands, H. W. *T. R.: The Last Romantic*. New York: Basic Books, 1997.

Brinkley, Alan. *American History*, 8th edition. New York: McGraw-Hill, 1991.

Carter, Susan B., Scott Sigmund Gartner, Michael R. Haines, Alan L. Olmstead, Richard Sutch, Gavin Wright, editors. *Historical Statistics of the United States*. New York: Cambridge University Press, 2006.

Cordery, Stacy A. *Alice: Alice Roosevelt Longworth from White House Princess to Washington Power Broker*. New York: Viking, 2007.

Dalton, Kathleen. *Theodore Roosevelt: A Strenuous Life*. New York: Random House, 2002.

Eyewitnesstohistory.com. http://www.eyewitnesstohistory.com/trwhitehouse.htm.

Harbaugh, William Henry. *Power and Responsibility: The Life and Times of Theodore Roosevelt.* New York: Farrar, Straus, and Cudahy, 1961.

Kraft, Betsy Harvey. *Theodore Roosevelt: Champion of the Human Spirit.* New York: Clarion Books, 2003.

McCullough, David. *Mornings on Horseback.* New York: Simon and Schuster, 1981.

Miller, Nathan. *Theodore Roosevelt: A Life.* New York: William Morrow, 1992.

Morris, Edmund. *The Rise of Theodore Roosevelt.* New York: Modern Library, 2001.

———. *Theodore Rex.* New York: Modern Library, 2002.

Mowry, George E. *The Era of Theodore Roosevelt and the Birth of Modern America, 1900–1912.* New York: Harper and Brothers, 1958.

Neiberg, Michael S. *Fighting the Great War: A Global History.* Cambridge, Mass.: Harvard University Press, 2005.

Online Highways. Sedition Act of 1918. http://www.u-s-history.com/pages/h1345.html.

Pringle, Henry F. *Theodore Roosevelt: A Biography.* New York: Harcourt, Brace and Company, 1931.

Roosevelt, Theodore. *Theodore Roosevelt: An Autobiography.* New York: De Capo Press, 1985.

Swainson, Bill, editor. *Encarta Book of Quotations.* New York: St. Martin's Press, 2000.

Wagenknecht, Edward. *The Seven Worlds of Theodore Roosevelt.* New York: Longmans, Green and Company, 1958.

INDEX